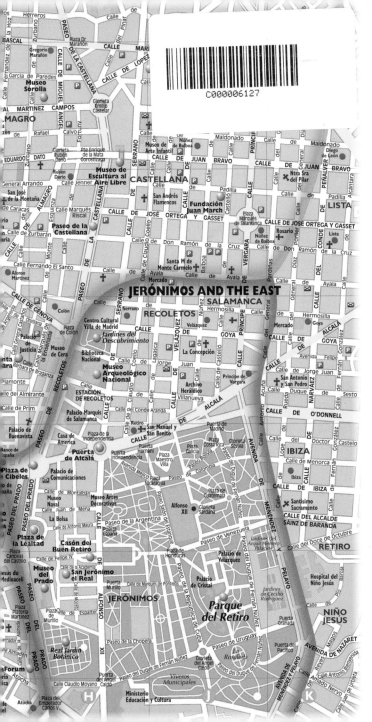

JERÓNIMOS AND THE EAST

CITYPACK GUIDE TO
Madrid

How to Use This Book

KEY TO SYMBOLS

✚ Map reference to the accompanying fold-out map

✉ Address

☎ Telephone number

🕐 Opening/closing times

🍴 Restaurant or café

🚆 Nearest rail station

🚇 Nearest subway (Metro) station

🚌 Nearest bus route

⛴ Nearest riverboat or ferry stop

♿ Facilities for visitors with disabilities

❓ Other practical information

▷ Further information

ℹ Tourist information

✋ Admission charges: Expensive (over €8), Moderate (€5–€8) and Inexpensive (€5 or less)

This guide is divided into four sections

• Essential Madrid: An introduction to the city and tips on making the most of your stay.

• Madrid by Area: We've broken the city into five areas, and recommended the best sights, shops, entertainment venues, nightlife and restaurants in each one. Suggested walks help you to explore on foot.

• Where to Stay: The best hotels, whether you're looking for luxury, budget or something in between.

• Need to Know: The info you need to make your trip run smoothly, including getting about by public transport, weather tips, emergency phone numbers and useful websites.

Navigation In the Madrid by Area chapter, we've given each area its own color, which is also used on the locator maps throughout the book and the map on the inside front cover.

Maps The fold-out map accompanying this book is a comprehensive street plan of Madrid. The grid on this fold-out map is the same as the grid on the locator maps within the book. We've given grid references within the book for each sight and listing.

Contents

CONTENTS

3

Introducing Madrid

In 1561, King Felipe II made Madrid capital of what soon became the world's biggest empire. Today, the grandeur remains: churches and museums, palaces and parks. But there are also medieval lanes and modern skyscrapers. That's why Madrid is unique.

Nowhere else in the world is the past so close to the present. Nuns and monks still live and worship in convents and monasteries that date back for centuries. Shops still make traditional cakes and breads; locals stop for olives and a small glass of wine in the way that their forebears have done for many years. But Madrid is also a city known for its exciting modern architecture, for its trendy small hotels, for its nightlife, with bars and clubs open till dawn…and even later at weekends. While thousands flock to watch the traditional rites at the world's most famous bullring, even more fans head for the Estadio Santiago Bernabéu to watch Real Madrid, arguably the most famous football club in the world.

No other city on the planet has three art galleries of such high quality within a few minutes' walk of each other. But Madrid has dozens of smaller museums that are less crowded and give an insight into the glory and grandeur that was imperial Spain. And it is all so walkable. Stroll around or, if your feet complain, take one of the cleanest, safest and cheapest public transport systems in the world. It is easy to get anywhere in minutes.

This is a city where you need to go with the flow. Only a foreigner eats dinner as early as nine at night here; only a foreigner walks the boiling pavements on a baking hot afternoon in high summer; only a foreigner spends a whole evening at the same tapas bar. So do as locals do: try different tapas at different bars, head out into the city for dinner at 10pm, take an afternoon nap, then stay up to the small hours.

Facts + Figures

- The population of Madrid is 3.3 million.
- Madrid is Europe's third-largest city, after London and Berlin.
- Madrid is the highest capital in Europe (646m/2,120ft).

SIMPLY THE BEST

FIFA, football's governing body, recognized Real Madrid as the world's best football club of the 20th century. You can tour their stadium, named for their former president, Santiago Bernabéu. He was part of a commission set up to promote a new competition—the European Cup. Real Madrid won the first ever European Cup on 13th June, 1956.

CAPITAL CITY

Madrid may be the capital of Spain but this is by name only. The city is locked in a perennial rivalry with equally self-important Barcelona for the honor of being cultural and sporting capital of the country. The two cities are constantly striving to outbid each other in the international events they stage and with their cutting-edge architecture.

MOVIE MAGIC

Acclaimed Spanish cinema director Pedro Almodóvar has always derived great inspiration from his home city. Many of his films, including *Women on the Verge of a Nervous Breakdown* (1988), nominated for an Oscar, are set in Madrid. *Labyrinth of Passion* (1982) was partly shot in the Rastro street market where Almodóvar once had a stand.

A Short Stay in Madrid

DAY 1

Morning To beat the crowds in the city's three great museums, you need a prompt start. For the **Museo Nacional Reina Sofía** (▷ 47), use the new extension entrance to the museum (off the Glorieta de Carlos V), still undiscovered by the main rush. Go straight up to see Picasso's *Guernica*, then work your way down.

Lunch When the museum gets busy, take the Metro across to Serrano for a smart lunch at **Sula Álbora** (▷ 80) or any of the myriad cafés.

Afternoon Now hit the shops. Work your way up Serrano to the **ABC Serrano Shopping Center** (▷ 92), a gallery of smart boutiques. Stroll down the streets called Goya, Velázquez and Ortega y Gasset. Then go back to your hotel for a siesta.

Evening Linger over tapas in the bars on and around the Plaza de Santa Ana. As well as traditional haunts, such as the Cervecería Alemana, there are contemporary wine bars, such as the **Vinoteca Barbechera** (▷ 66). Stroll down to the **Museo Thyssen-Bornemisza** (▷ 48) and soak up some culture. In July and August, the museum stays open late during *Noches de verano*, Summer Nights.

Dinner Afterward, still in the Museo Thyssen-Bornemisza, dine at the **El Mirador del Museo restaurant**, on the terrace, high above the city.

Later The Spanish love to stay up late, late, late. Hit a popular club such as the **Café Central** (▷ 63) for jazz or the **Casa Patas** (▷ 63) for flamenco. And if you are still going strong at 4am, join the locals at **Chocolatería San Ginés** (▷ 65) for hot chocolate before heading for bed.

DAY 2

Morning If it is a Sunday morning, then do what everyone does: go to El Rastro (▷ 53). This swirling mix of outdoor markets and shops has everything from cheap toys, pottery and clothing to expensive antiques and leather goods. Make sure that you have no tempting bag or wallet on view. Afterward, drift through the narrow lanes toward the **Plaza de Tirso de Molina**, with its cheerful flower stands, smart new paving, fountains and statue of Tirso de Molina himself. The real name of this playwright was Gabriel Tellez, and he is best remembered for his character, Don Juan. Stroll on east through the old city streets and join locals grazing along Calle de Jésus at tapas bars such as **Cervecería Cervantes** (▷ 65).

Lunch Instead of a big meal, continue hopping in and out of the line of tapas bars along the street. Have dessert at **La Esquina del Café** (▷ 65).

Afternoon Cross the Paseo del Prado and watch *madrileños* at play in **Parque del Retiro** (▷ 73). There are puppet shows for little children; boats for hire on the lake; and live concerts in summer, when most people are happy to stretch out on the lawns and snooze.

Evening Another authentic Madrid experience is the *zarzuela*. Part Gilbert & Sullivan, part Feydeau farce, these are Spanish comic operas. The music is jolly, the plots are silly, so you don't need to understand the language. The **Teatro de la Zarzuela** (▷ 64) also stages ballet and dance.

Dinner To keep the Spanish experience going to the end of your day, dine nearby at **Taberna Maceira** (▷ 66), where crowds of locals and visitors alike pack in elbow-to-elbow at wooden tables for simple, hearty, Galician dishes.

ESSENTIAL MADRID TOP 25

▶ ▶ ▶

These pages are a quick guide to the Top 25, which are described in more detail later. Here they are listed alphabetically, and the tinted background shows which area they are in.

CHUECA AND THE NORTH 81–94

EL VISO

Parque Santa Engracia

RÍOS ROSAS

CHAMBERÍ

RAFALGAR

Museo Sorolla

Museo Lázaro Galdiano

ALMAGRO

CASTELLANA

LISTA

SALAMANCA

JUSTICIA

Jardines del Descubrimiento

RECOLETOS

JERÓNIMOS AND THE EAST 67–80

GOYA

Monasterio de las Descalzas Reales

SOL

Real Academia de Bellas Artes

Plaza de la Cibeles

Puerta de Alcalá

IBIZA

Puerta del Sol

CORTES

Museo Thyssen-Bornemisza

Museo del Prado

Jardines del Arquit Herrero Palacios

RETIRO

CENTRO

JERÓNIMOS

Jardines de Cecilio Rodríguez

NIÑO JESÚS

CENTRO 43–66

Real Jardín Botánico

Parque del Retiro

La Rosaleda

Museo Nacional Reina Sofía

Viveros Municipales

MBAJADORES

PACÍFICO

ESSENTIAL MADRID TOP 25

9

Shopping

Since the 1980s, out-of-town malls have sprung up and international chains have crept in. But fears that late 20th-century shopping practices would kill off Madrid's many unique little stores have been largely unfounded, and the range of shopping experiences available for visitors is wonderfully diverse. It's these contrasts between the best on the international scene and some superbly idiosyncratic outlets that make Madrid shopping so serendipitous.

A Bit of Everything

It's not just what shops sell that provides a contrast—how they look is also varied. Temples of consumerism in steel and glass happily rub shoulders with cramped, dark shops where the stock is piled high and the merchandise specialized beyond belief. Few other world capitals have as many stores devoted to so many oddities—outsize corsetry, plaster statuary, crystallized violets. This gives Madrid shopping a special appeal, whether you're after easy-to-carry souvenirs or seriously self-indulgent retail therapy, or you simply enjoy window-shopping.

Clothes and Accessories

Madrid has branches of some of Spain and Europe's best-known fashion stores, as well

---

WHERE TO SHOP

Ask a *madrileño* where to find the city's shopping heart and the answer is bound to be around Calle Preciados, the pedestrianized drag that connects Puerta del Sol with the Gran Vía. Here you'll find branches of all the big chain stores, as well as Madrid's biggest department store, and everything from fashion to food. Smarter by far are the quiet, well-heeled streets of the Salamanca district, home to the big designer names and luxury stores of all description. The best places to trawl for souvenirs are around the Plaza Mayor and the surrounding Los Austrias district, or Malasaña. Head to Chueca for cutting-edge style and street fashion.

Flamenco shop; designer store; flea market; legs of ham (top to bottom)

as the latest in the stylish chain-store fashion for which Spain is renowned. Spanish leather shoes, bags and belts are some of the best in Europe, and excellent value.

Gifts

For gifts, you'll find goods from all over Spain, ranging from the tasteful fringed and embroidered shawls and mantillas, warm winter capes, elegant hats, delicate china, traditional ceramics and damascene work, to the marvellously tacky (plastic flamenco dolls, a poster of a *torero* with your name on it, and metal Don Quixotes).

Food

Food makes a great souvenir or gift. In addition to the obvious olive oil, nougat or chocolate, hunt down saffron, and the wonderful dried nuts, seeds and fruits so loved by the Spanish. Or look for convent-baked biscuits or cakes, vacuum-packed *jamón* (dry-cured ham), *chorizo* (spicy sausage) or *morcilla* (unctuous black pudding).

Tax Refunds and Sales

IVA (sales tax) is added at seven percent on food and 18 percent on most other items. Non-EU visitors can reclaim the IVA on purchases, but the total must be at least €90.15, paid in a single store in a single day. Stores taking part display a Tax-Free shopping sticker. For more detailed information, see www.okspain.org. Sales generally run from mid-January to February, and July to August.

Flea market; lace fans; shop window (top to bottom)

MARKETS

Markets are not only a window into everyday life, but also the perfect place to pick up a picnic to eat in the park. Some of the best are La Cebada (🚇 La Latina)—for a huge range of goods and low prices; El Rastro (🚇 Tirso de Molina)—the famous Sunday market; and La Paz (🚇 Serrano)—quality and varied produce aimed at the prosperous Salamanca inhabitants.

Shopping by Theme

Whether you're looking for a department store, a quirky boutique, or something in between, you'll find it all in Madrid. On this page shops are listed by theme. For a more detailed write-up, see the individual listings in Madrid by Area.

ALL UNDER ONE ROOF

ABC Serrano Shopping Center (▷ 92)
Centro Comercial Príncipe Pío (▷ 39)
El Corte Inglés (▷ 61)
FNAC (▷ 61)
El Jardín de Serrano (▷ 78)
Mercado de Fuencarral (▷ 92)
VIPS (▷ 62)

ANTIQUES AND GIFTS

Felix Antigüedades (▷ 61)
Galería de Arte Victoria Hidalgo (▷ 78)
Galerías Piquér (▷ 62)
Museo del Prado (▷ 78)
Museo del Traje (▷ 39)
Stamps and Coins Market (▷ 62)

FASHION/ ACCESSORIES

Fabendi (▷ 78)
Massimo Dutti Woman (▷ 39)
Pull & Bear (▷ 39)
Purificación García (▷ 92)
Trucco (▷ 39)
Zara (▷ 62)

FOOD AND WINE

Antigua Pastelería del Pozo (▷ 61)
Cacao Sampaka (▷ 92)
Mariano Madrueño (▷ 62)
Reserva y Cata (▷ 92)

SHOES/ ACCESSORIES

La Violeta (▷ 62)
Guantes Luque (▷ 62)
Ioli (▷ 92)
Lurueña (▷ 39)
Tino González (▷ 39)

SOMETHING DIFFERENT

Berbería del Sahara y El Sahel (▷ 39)
Coronel Tapiocca (▷ 78)
El Flamenco Vive (▷ 61)
Homeless (▷ 92)
Imaginarium (▷ 78)
Natura Selection (▷ 78)
Perfumería Alvarez Gomez (▷ 78)
Piel de Toro (▷ 78)
Toni Martin (▷ 39)

TRADITIONAL

Amparo Mercería (▷ 61)
Antigua Casa Talavera (▷ 61)
Casa de Diego (▷ 61)
La Favorita (▷ 61)
Guitarras Ramírez (▷ 62)
Seseña (▷ 62)

Madrid by Night

Madrid has a year-round agenda of cultural evening events, from opera, orchestral concerts, plays, dance and original-language films to jazz, flamenco and Latin American music. Get information in the weekly entertainment guide *Guía del Ocio* and reserve tickets for concerts and plays via www.entradas.com or try Localidades Galicia (www.bullfightticketsmadrid.com; tel 91531 27 32) for bullfight tickets.

A Quiet Evening

With little hope of a restaurant dinner before 9, you might want to take your evening stroll before you eat. Touristy though it is, the Plaza Mayor looks great by night; from here you can wander through buzzing Huertas down to the Paseo del Prado, a wonderful place in summer for a stroll and a drink at a terraza. A few minutes' walk away lies the Retiro Park, perfect on balmy evenings. For window shopping, head for the elegant streets of Salamanca or lively Chueca.

Night Owls

Madrid's reputation as an all-night party town is deserved. Nightlife concentrates around Huertas, Lavapiés, Malasaña and off Sol. Gay-oriented Chueca is ultra cool and Salamanca is for a dressed-up occasion. But be warned: don't go out too early or you might think there is no action. A night out in Madrid can start at 10 or 11pm, after dinner, or even later, particularly on weekends and in the summer.

FLOODLIT STONE

Great cities look wonderful under floodlights and Madrid is no exception. Imaginative lighting enhances much of the city after dark. Don't miss the subtly lit charms of the Plaza Mayor, then enjoy the brilliance lighting adds to the Palacio Real and the Plaza de Oriente. The Paseo del Prado is beautifully illuminated at night; admire the sparkle of light on the water of the fountains in Plaza de la Cibeles and Plaza de Canovas de Castillo before stopping at one of the summertime *terrazas*.

Flamenco show; musicians performing; flamenco dancer; taberna sign (top to bottom)

Eating Out

You can eat regional food from all over the peninsula in Madrid, as well as superb tapas, snacks and dishes from farther afield.

Where to Eat
There's a huge choice of eating places in Madrid, particularly around Sol, Santa Ana and Huertas, and the Latina, Lavapiés, Chueca and Malasaña districts. The city's smartest and priciest restaurants are concentrated near the Paseo del Prado and the Retiro and scattered throughout Salamanca. The IVA tax of seven percent is added to bills in restaurants and bars. As for tipping, service is included; however it is customary to leave a few coins in a bar and five percent in a restaurant.

Types of Restaurant
Restaurantes are officially graded with one to five forks, and range from simple establishments serving up the trusty *menú del día* to very grand—and pricey—venues. Tapas bars are quintessentially Spanish. These snacks range from a few olives or almonds to tortillas, shellfish, meat croquettes and wonderful vegetable dishes laced with garlic. All tapas bars have their own special dishes, and locals move from place to place, ordering the dishes that each bar does particularly well. The barman normally keeps track of what you've had to eat, and you pay at the end. The city has a very active café life, with some wonderful old places where you can read the papers and watch the world go by.

MEAL TIMES
The Spanish usually eat breakfast (*desayuno*) between 9 and 10, though it is served earlier in hotels. It's usually sweet—*chocolate con churros* (hot chocolate and stick-shaped doughnuts) or toast with jam. Traditionally, the main meal of the day, lunch (*almuerzo*) is from 2 to 4. The Spanish eat dinner (*cena*) any time after 9.30 through till midnight. But, with cafés and tapas bars open long hours, you can always find something tasty to eat.

Tapas bar; pinchos; taberna; tapas dishes (top to bottom)

Restaurants by Cuisine

There are restaurants to suit all tastes and budgets in Madrid. On this page they are listed by cuisine. For a more detailed description of each restaurant, see Madrid by Area.

BASQUE AND CATALAN

Dantxari (▷ 41)
Errota-Zar (▷ 65)
Lazema (▷ 41)
Taberna del Alabardero (▷ 42)

COFFEE, TEA, CHOCOLATE AND ICE CREAM

Chocolatería San Ginés (▷ 65)
La Esquina del Café (▷ 65)
Ritz Hotel (▷ 80)

GALICIAN AND ASTURIAN

A'Casiña (▷ 41)
Casa Mingo (▷ 41)
La Hoja (▷ 80)
Restaurante Moaña (▷ 66)
Taberna Maceira (▷ 66)

NATIONAL AND INTERNATIONAL

La Castela (▷ 79)
La Gamella (▷ 79)
Indice Restaurant at AC Palacio del Retiro (▷ 80)
Pedro Larumbe (▷ 94)
Restaurante Viridiana (▷ 80)
La Sacristía (▷ 94)
Sula Álbora (▷ 80)
La Taquería de Birra (▷ 42)
Trattoria Sant'Arcangelo (▷ 80)

SPANISH

El Bierzo (▷ 94)
El Botánico (▷ 79)
Casa Manolo (▷ 94)
El Ingenio (▷ 41)
Mercado de San Antón (▷ 94)
Mesón Cinco Jotas (▷ 42)
Prada a Tope (▷ 42)

Sal Gorda (▷ 42)
El Senador (▷ 42)
La Taurina (▷ 66)
Viuda de Vacas (▷ 66)

TAPAS

Baztán (▷ 94)
Los Caracoles (▷ 65)
Casa Alberto (▷ 65)
Casa Labra (▷ 65)
Cervecería Cervantes (▷ 65)
Lhardy (▷ 65)
Sanlúcar (▷ 42)
Taberna de Antonio Sánchez (▷ 66)
Vinoteca Barbechera (▷ 66)

TRADITIONAL MADRID CUISINE

La Bola Taberna (▷ 41)
Botín (▷ 65)
Café de Oriente (▷ 41)
El Molino de Los Porches (▷ 42)
Posada de la Villa (▷ 66)

Top Tips For...

Whatever your special interest while you are in Madrid, these suggestions should help you to make the most of your visit. Each sight or listing has more details later on in the book.

PEOPLE-WATCHING

Café de Oriente (▷ 41): next to the Opera House, facing the Royal Palace.
Plaza Mayor: for architecture, murals, statues (▷ 51).
Retiro park lake: in a rowing boat (▷ 73).
Teleférico **(cable car):** on the way to or from the Casa de Campo (▷ 34).

SHOPPING TILL YOU DROP

ABC Serrano: A small and classy mall in the heart of an up-market shopping area (▷ 92).
El Rastro: the fun Sunday morning market (▷ 53).
El Corte Inglés: Spain's top department store (▷ 61).
Mercado de Fuencarral: funky and fun (▷ 92).

Teleférico; shopping spree (above)

CHECKING OUT GREAT ART

The Prado: for Goya's greatest works (▷ 70).
Museo Nacional Reina Sofía: for Picasso's *Guernica* (▷ 47).
Museo Thyssen-Bornemisza: for 19th-century American art (▷ 48).

SPLASHING OUT

Genuine antiques: in the Galerías Piquér (▷ 62).
Fine ceramics: Antigua Casa Talavera (▷ 61).
A real fan: Casa de Diego (▷ 61).

The view of the Palacio de Cristal across the lake in El Retiro Park (above right); eye-catching fans (right)

Flamenco show (below)

BEING ENTERTAINED

Flamenco: at a dozen clubs, such as Casa Patas (▷ 63) or Corral de la Morería (▷ 40), a legendary *tablao*-restaurant.
Football: at Real Madrid (▷ 100), Atlético de Madrid, Rayo Vallecano.
Jazz: at the Café Central (▷ 63).

KEEPING KIDS HAPPY

Carriage ride: tour the park by horse-drawn carriage (▷ 73).
Casa de Campo: go to the Parque de Atracciones fairground (▷ 24).
Museo del Traje: dress up in 18th-century garb (▷ 31).
Playgrounds: let off steam in renovated plazas, such as the Plaza de Santa Ana (▷ 59).

KEEPING TO A TIGHT BUDGET

Concerts: check out free concerts in the Retiro park (▷ 73).
Festivals: ask at the tourist office if there are any parades or processions.
Free entry: visit museums on their weekly free entrance days.
Museo de Escultura al Aire Libre: great sculpture free at the outdoor sculpture museum (▷ 88).

Casa de Campo; flamingos in the zoo at Casa de Campo (above)

TRADITIONAL TAPAS

Baztán (▷ 94).
Taberna de Antonio Sánchez (▷ 66).
Los Caracoles (▷ 65).
Sanlúcar (▷ 42).

Selection of tapas (left)

OLD-FASHIONED FEASTING

Restaurante Botín; stay in a funky hotel (below)

Botín: the world's oldest restaurant (▷ 65).
Taberna Maceira: Galician cooking, especially *pulpo* (octopus) (▷ 66).
Restaurante Moaña: fish and seafood in a formal setting (▷ 66).
Posada de la Villa: traditional Madrid oven-roast lamb (▷ 66).

FUNKY HOTELS

Hospes: a new boutique hotel in a classic building (▷ 112).
ME Madrid: was the posh old Reina Victoria, now hip and happening (▷ 112).
Petit Palace: in the swish part of town, on top of the best window-shopping around (▷ 112).
Quo: a new group of funky hotels in the city (▷ 112).

CELEB-SPOTTING

La Bardemcilla (Augusto Figueroa 47), once owned by film stars Monica and Javier Bardem, and still pulling in the stars.
Bar Skynight, on top of the Hotel Puerta América (Avenida de América) (▷ 112).
Fortuny, once a palace, still glitzy (▷ 93).
Glass Bar at the posh Hotel Urban (▷ 64).

Cocktails (above)

PARTYING TILL DAWN

Ojalá Awareness Club: the indoor beach is a must (▷ 93).
Marula Café: live DJs and funk at this all-night venue (▷ 40).
Kapital: seven floors of fun at Madrid's biggest club (▷ 79).

Dancing in a club (right)

The Royal Palace is now a museum, but this area retains the elegance of the past. There are also plenty of green spaces.

Palacio and the West

Plaza
Cristo Rey

P

CALLE ISAAC PERAL

P

Calle de Hilarión Eslava

CALLE DE URQUIJO

Argüelles

Mercado
LA

CALLE ALBERTO AGUILERA

Servicio
Histórico
del Ejército

CALLE PRINCESA

UNIVERSIDAD

Centro
Cultural
Conde
Duque

Ventura
Rodríguez

Plaza
Cristino
Martos

Torre de
Madrid

Templo de
Debod

Museo
Cerralbo

Plaza de
España
Monumento a
Cervantes

GRAN

VIA

Plaza de
España

Palacio
del Senado

SAN VICENTE

BAILEN

Calle de Torija

Santo
Domingo

CUESTA DE

Jardines
de Sabatini

Monasterio de la
Encarnación

Campo
del Moro

Palacio
Real

Plaza de
Oriente

Calle de Arrieta

Opera

PALACIO

Plaza
de la
Armería

Teatro
Real

Catedral
de la Almudena

BAILEN

San Nicolás
de los Servitas

Muralla
Arabe

Plasencia

Parque Emir
Mohamed I

DE

SEGOVIA

Viaducto

CALLE

Plaza
Granado

Parque de
las Vistillas

Capilla
Cristo de
los Dolores

Calle Don Pedro

Plaza
San
Francisco

Jardines de
las Vistillas

GRAN VIA DE SAN FRANCISCO

Basílica de
San Francisco
el Grande

RONDA DE SAN FRANCISCO

PASEO IMPERIAL

E

F

G

Casa de Campo

**TOP
25**

Flamingos in the zoo (left); running in Casa de Campo (right)

THE BASICS

➕ A6
✉ Calle Marqués de Monistrol, Avenida de Portugal
🚇 Lago, Batán, Casa de Campo
🚌 25, 33, 65

Parque de Atracciones
www.parquedeatracciones.es
➕ Off map at A7
🕐 Jun to mid-Sep daily noon–dusk; mid-Sep to Mar Sat–Sun noon–dusk; Easter week daily noon–dusk; Apr Fri–Sun noon–dusk; May Tue–Sun noon–dusk
🍴 Cafés, restaurants
🚇 Batán
🚌 33, 65
♿ Good
💲 Expensive

Zoo-Aquarium de Madrid
www.zoomadrid.com
➕ Off map at A7
🕐 Mon–Fri 11–dusk, Sat–Sun 10.30–dusk
🍴 Cafés, restaurants
🚇 Batán, Casa de Campo
🚌 33 ♿ Good
💲 Expensive

TIP

● Take the 11-minute cable car trip from Parque del Oeste (▷ 34) for superb views over the city.

That Madrid is one of Europe's greenest capitals is mainly because of the 1,722ha (4,255-acre) Casa de Campo, 'the lungs of Madrid', stretching away to the north-west. Once a royal hunting estate, it was opened to the public in 1931, quickly becoming popular as a cool haven in Madrid's hot summer.

Wide open space In Casa de Campo, you can walk for a couple of hours without being interrupted (though this is best avoided after dark). During the Civil War, Franco's troops were based here, and signs of trenches are still visible. The park contains sports facilities, a large lake (where you can hire boats), amusement park, aquarium and zoo. The teleférico (cable car, www.teleferico.com) runs up here from the Parque del Oeste (▷ 34), and the 11-minute journey is an excellent way to arrive, affording superb views over the city.

Parque de Atracciones This amusement park has more than 40 rides, from gentle merry-go-rounds to the stomach-churning Top Spin and the breathtaking Tornado rollercoaster. There are open-air concerts in summer.

The zoo Madrid's zoo is one of the best in Europe. It contains over 5,000 animals and more than 100 species of bird. There is a dolphinarium, a train ride, an aquarium and a children's section. Parrot shows, the tank of sharks and birds of prey are all popular.

Catedral de la Almudena

Though not the loveliest cathedral, it reflects years of Spanish architectural thought. The mixture of styles shows how relaxed *madrileños* have been about this building, which you would expect to have been a priority.

A long delay Just 20 years ago, Madrid lacked a cathedral, incredible though it may seem. The first plans for the Almudena, constructed on what was formerly the site of Muslim Madrid's principal mosque, were drawn up in 1879 under Alfonso XII by the architect Giambattista Sacchetti. Redesigned in 1883, it is based on the pattern of a 13th-century cathedral, with a chancel similar to the one at Rheims. A neo-classical style was introduced into the design in 1944, but it wasn't until 1993 that the cathedral was consecrated by the Pope. The main entrance is opposite the Royal Palace, the entrance to the crypt along La Cuesta de la Vega.

The story of the Almudena Virgin According to legend, the image of the Virgin over the entrance had been hidden in the 11th century by Mozarabs. When Spanish hero El Cid recon-quered Madrid, he ordered that the image be found, but without success. Alfonso VI then instructed his troops and the people of Madrid to dismantle the city walls to find the image. When they reached the grain deposits, they heard a noise from the turrets above, which then collapsed, revealing an image of the Virgin and Child.

THE BASICS

➕ E7
✉ Calle Bailén. Next to Palacio Real
☎ 91 542 22 00
🕐 Daily 9–8.30
Ⓜ Ópera
🚌 3, 31, 148
♿ Good
🎫 Free

HIGHLIGHTS

● Virgin of Almudena
● Coffin of San Isidro
● Dome 20m (66ft) in diameter
● Grenzing organ
● The 104m (340ft)-long nave
● 12 statues of the apostles
● Bronze doors

Ermita de San Antonio de la Florida

The facade of the hermitage (left); the exterior (right)

THE BASICS

www.esmadrid.com

🔗 C6

✉ Glorieta de San Antonio de la Florida 5

☎ 91 542 07 22

🕐 Tue–Fri 10–8, Sat, Sun 10–2. Closed public hols

🚇 Príncipe Pío

🚉 Príncipe Pío

🚌 41, 46, 75

♿ None

🎟 Free

HIGHLIGHTS

● Cupola
● Balustrade
● Marble and stucco font (1798)
● *Lápida de Goya*
● Mirrors under the cupola
● High altar
● Lamp under the cupola (18th century)
● *Inmaculada*, Jacinto Gómez Pastor
● *San Luis and San Isidro*, Jacinto Gómez Pastor

Goya is surely the painter that most *madrileños* want to claim as their own. The San Antonio de la Florida Hermitage, a National Monument, is a fine memorial to his memory.

Resting place Both church and hermitage—the latter to the left as you face the two buildings—are off the beaten track, but worthwhile both for their intimacy and to view Goya's frescoes. The original hermitage was begun in 1792 by Charles IV's Italian architect, Francisco Fontana. Goya's remains were buried here in 1919, but without his head: it is said that it was stolen by scientists who wished to study it.

The frescoes Painted using a technique that was revolutionary at the time, the frescoes are distinguished by their richness of color. They tell the life of St. Anthony, representing the saint raising a murdered man from the dead to enable him to name his murderer and spare the life of the innocent accused. The models for the frescoes were members of the Spanish Court, but include other less reputable figures—placing rogues alongside the Court officials has been seen as indicating Goya's contempt for the Court of the time.

Girlfriends and boyfriends St. Anthony is the patron saint of sweethearts, and every 13 June girls come here to pray for a boyfriend. Thirteen pins are placed inside the font; then a girl puts her hand in and the number of pins that stick indicates how many beaux she will have that year.

The Monastery of the Incarnation (left); St. Teresa in stained glass (right)

Located away from the traffic of Calle Bailén, the Monastery of the Incarnation is suffused with religious calm that brings peace to the soul.

History Designed by Juan Gómez de Mora in 1611 on instructions from Queen Margarita, wife of Philip III, the church in the Royal Monastery is typical of Habsburg Spanish religious architecture. Originally the monastery was connected by a passage to the Arab fortress where the Royal Palace now stands. The church was damaged by fire in 1734, and reconstructed in classical-baroque style; the granite facade is all that remains of the original. A 45-minute guided tour leads you through the monastery, which is still used by nuns of the Augustine order; you see the Royal Room, hung with uninspired portraits of the royal family, and one of Madrid's most beautiful churches, the monastery church, which includes a reliquary. Here, also, is the monastery museum.

The Reliquary In the middle of the church stand an altar and altarpiece depicting the Holy Family by Bernadino Luini, a pupil of Leonardo da Vinci, and an ornate tabernacle in bronze and rock crystal. Inside is a crucifix of Christ with a crown of thorns, oddly charred: tradition holds that these are the remains of a crucifix defiled by heretics. Among the 1,500 relics on display, in a small glass globe to the right of the door as you enter, is the dried blood of St. Pantaleón, which is said to mysteriously liquify every year on 27 July, St. Pantaleón's Day.

THE BASICS

www.patrimonionacional.es
➕ E7
✉ Plaza de la Encarnación 1
☎ 91 454 88 00
🕐 Monastery and Reliquary: Tue–Sat 10–2, 4–6.30, Sun 10–3
Ⓜ Ópera
🚌 25, 39, 148
♿ None
💶 Moderate

HIGHLIGHTS

- *John the Baptist,* Jusepe Ribera
- *Handing over of the Princesses,* anonymous painting in lobby
- *Recumbent Christ,* Perronius
- Royal Room
- Altarpiece
- Cupola, with frescoes by González Velázquez
- Frescoes: Francisco Bayeu
- Charred crucifix
- Blood of St. Pantaleón

Museo Cerralbo

HIGHLIGHTS

● Grand staircase
● *Ecstasy of St. Francis*,
El Greco
● *Jacob with his Flock*, José
de Ribera
● *Devotion*, Alonso Cano
● *Immaculate Conception*,
Francisco Zurbarán
● *Porcupines and Snakes*,
Frans Snyders
● Sword collection from the
courts of Louis XV and XVI
● Monumental mystery clock

TIP

● Audioguides, in English,
are available and informative.

Idiosyncratic and intermittently splendid, this curiosity gives you an indication of how the nobility of Madrid lived 100 years ago, in particular the extravagant and fascinating Marquis de Cerralbo.

Home life When you see the two-floor, late 19th-century home of the 17th Marquis of Cerralbo from the outside it looks rather unpromising. But the clutter of artifacts inside is quite fascinating, and, uniquely among the house-museums in Madrid, the collections are rivaled by the architecture and decor of the rooms themselves, ranging from the frankly shabby to the magnificent. Politician, man of letters and collector, the Marquis donated the house and its contents to the state in 1922, stipulating that his collection be displayed exactly as he had left it. This is a

The grand staircase (left); the mirrored ballroom (right)

unique opportunity to see a near-intact aristocrat's home of the turn of the 20th century.

The collection A magnificent grand staircase by Soriano Fort is to your right as you enter. On the second floor, the most notable exhibit is El Greco's striking *Ecstasy of St. Francis* (1600–05) in the chapel. In the gallery surrounding the patio, there are works by José de Ribera and Alonso Cano, as well as haunting Alessandro Magnasco landscapes. On the third floor there are collections of Western and oriental weaponry, a dining room containing a remarkable Frans Snyders painting, and an appealingly homey library. Pride of place is given to the sumptuous mirrored ballroom on the first floor, which displays the Marquis' Saxon porcelain, as well as intricate clocks, including one particularly fascinating and huge specimen.

THE BASICS

http://museocerralbo.mcu.es

🚩 E6

✉ Calle Ventura Rodríguez 17

☎ 91 547 36 46

🕐 Mon–Wed, Fri–Sat 9.30–3, Thu 5–8pm, Sun 10–3

Ⓜ Ventura Rodríguez, Plaza de España

🚌 1, 2, 44, 46, 74, 133, C1, C2

♿ Moderate; call in advance of visit

🎟 Inexpensive. Free Sat 2–3pm and Thu

Museo de América

TOP 25

An equestrian statue set in the form of a tree trunk (right) at the American Museum (left)

HIGHLIGHTS

- Canoe and tepee (Area 3)
- Statues of tribal chieftains (Area 3)
- Painting of *Entrance of Viceroy Morcillo into Potosí* (Area 3)
- Shrunken heads (Area 4)
- Mummy of Parácas (Area 4)
- Treasure of the Quimbayas (Area 4)
- 'Day of the Dead' paraphernalia (Area 4)
- Trocortesiano Maya Codex (Area 5)

This attractive museum can be seen either as an attempt to promote international understanding or as propaganda for the Spanish Conquest. Still, it makes a unique contribution to Spanish culture.

History Devoted to the presentation and explication of pre-Columbian and Hispanic artifacts from Latin America, the America Museum, on the edge of the sprawling University area, is the best place in Spain to absorb the flavor of the culture of a different continent. Gold drew the Spanish to South America and gold draws visitors to marvel at the skills of the pre-Columbian artists. Many art works were melted down, so what is on show is even more important. Indeed, many South Americans living and working in Madrid are among the visitors. On Thursdays, the restaurant even serves an array of tasty South American dishes, such as frijoles, soups, Cuban-style rice and beans, green beans with tomatoes and spicy spaghetti.

Layout It's best to follow the suggested route, as it is easy to get confused. The collection is spread over two floors and five areas with various themes: the tools of understanding, the reality of America's society, religion and communication. Two particular highlights are the Treasure of the Quimbayas (Area 4), including exquisite gold figures, skull-cap helmets, drinking flasks and trumpets from Colombia, and the Trocortesiano Maya Codex (Area 5), which records the arrival of the Spaniards in the New World and the Spanish Conquest in minute, intricate runes.

Museo del Traje

One of the men's costumes on display (right) at the Museum of Costume (left)

Since its opening in 2004, the Museum of Costume has made its mark on the Madrid cultural stage. Far more than just clothes, the collection is a reflection of how Spanish society has changed over the centuries.

The collection In the 14 galleries of this elegant museum, the clothes are shown at different angles, so that you can see the front of some, the back of others. Through the glass, you can peer at centuries-old frock coats and silk doublets, and admire the embroidery on bodices. A fraction of the collection's 21,000 items is on display. The galleries are organized chronologically, showing how fashion and practicality evolved over centuries. The most delicate pieces cannot be on display for long, so exhibits are routinely changed.

Hi-tech display Although historians are fascinated by the 13th-century trousseau of the daughter of Ferdinand III, most visitors are intrigued by a hi-tech display devoted to women's underwear. Virtual reality video twirls viewers from the bodices of the 17th century to the girdles of the 1940s. But there is everything in the museum, from Spanish mantillas to the latest shoes. Of course, with rooms all to themselves are Spain's legendary fashion designers, such as Mariano Fortuny (born in Granada) and Cristóbal Balenciaga, a Basque who went on to take the Parisian fashion world by storm. Best of all, you can try on old-fashioned clothes to get a feel of how comfortable—or uncomfortable—they were.

THE BASICS

www.museodeltraje.mcu.es

✚ C3

✉ Avenida Juan de Herrera 2

☎ 91 550 47 00

🕐 Tue–Sat 9.30–7, Sun and public hols 10–3

🍴 Café, restaurant

Ⓜ Moncloa, Ciudad Universitaria

🚌 46, 82, 83, 84, 132, 133

♿ Good

🎫 Inexpensive. Free to under 18s, over 65s; Sat after 2.30pm, Sun

HIGHLIGHTS

● The funerary apparel of Doña María, daughter of Fernando III
● 1740s silver frock coat
● Women's underwear
● Spanish headdresses
● Regional costume
● The genius of Fortuny
● Christian Dior clothes
● Pedro Rodríguez and the New Look
● The catwalk

TIPS

● Book up for a special meal at Lazema (▷ 41), the museum's own very posh restaurant. In summer, dine out on the terrace.
● Excellent shop, with high-quality silk ties, Spanish shawls and jewelry.

Palacio Real

HIGHLIGHTS

● Grand staircase
● Sala de Porcelana
● Salón de Alabarderos
● Salón de Columnas
● Sala de Gasparini
● Salón de Carlos III
● Clock collection
● Chapel by Giambattista
Sacchetti and Ventura
Rodríguez
● Music Museum
● Sabatini Gardens

TIP

● The Changing of the
Guard takes place at noon on
the first Wed of the month
(except Jul, Aug, Sep).

**The scale of the palace is awesome and
the pomp overwhelming. The story that
sentries guarding the rear of the building
used to freeze to death in the icy wind
adds to the sense of chilliness it inspires.**

Scaled to fit The Royal Palace was begun under
Philip V in 1737, after the old Muslim fortress was
destroyed by fire in 1734. The original design by
Filippo Juvanna was for facades measuring 475m
(520 yards) each, or three times longer than the
palace now, but there was neither the space nor
the money for that. It was completed in 1764, to
designs by Sacchetti. From the street side, it is a
normal palatial building of the period, with Ionic
pilasters framing the reception hall windows. The
royal family does not actually live here: it is used
occasionally for state visits, during which dinner is

The facade of the Palacio Real (left); statues lining the approach (middle); guards outside the palace (right); changing of the guard (bottom left); the exterior of the Royal Palace (bottom middle); a guard taking part in the changing of the guard ceremony (bottom right)

served in the gala dining room. The entrance is to the south side of the building, across the Plaza de la Armería, which is flanked by the Royal Armory housing El Cid's sword and the ornate armor of Carlos V and Felipe III.

Interior and gardens There are more than 3,000 rooms, and most are never used. A ceiling by Conrado Giaquinto accents the grand staircase. The stucco ceiling of the Sala de Gasparini is remarkable, while the ceiling of the Sala de Porcelana, built for Charles III, has a fine display of white, gold and green porcelain plaques. To the north of the palace are the elegant Sabatini Gardens, which offer the best view of the palace, while to the rear is the Campo del Moro. The only way to see the palace is by following a fixed itinerary, which takes in the finest rooms.

THE BASICS

www.patrimonionacional.es

➕ E7

✉ Calle Bailén

☎ 91 454 88 00

🕐 Apr–Sep daily 10–8, Oct–Mar daily 10–6. Closed during public events

Ⓜ Ópera

🚌 3, 25, 39, 148

♿ Very good

💲 Expensive. Free to under 5s

Parque del Oeste

The rose garden (left); remains of the Templo de Debod (right)

THE BASICS

🔲 C4

✉ Paseo Ruperto Chapi

☎ 91 548 95 12

🕐 Teleférico: Sat, Sun and public hols 12–6

🚇 Moncloa, Príncipe Pío, Plaza de España

🚌 21, 46, 74, 160, 161

Templo de Debod

www.esmadrid.com

✉ Calle de Ferraz 1, Parque de la Montaña

☎ 91 366 74 15

🕐 Apr–Sep Tue–Fri 10–2, 6–8, Sat, Sun 10–2; Oct–Mar Tue–Fri 9.45–1.45, 4.15–6.15, Sat, Sun 10–2. Closed Mon and public hols

🚇 Plaza de España, Ventura Rodríguez

🚌 1, 2, 44, 133, 138

🖐 Free

HIGHLIGHTS

● *Teleférico*
● La Rosaleda
● Fuente (fountain)
● Statue of Juan de Villanueva
● Statue of Sor Juana Inés de la Cruz
● Statue of Simón Bolívar
● View over Casa de Campo
● Trees, including atlas cedar, cypress and magnolia

Less frequented and more informal than the Retiro, the Parque del Oeste is the best place in the city for a peaceful stroll in summer, particularly at the quieter northern end. It is best avoided at night.

Rubbish dump to park Designed in the first years of the 20th century by landscape gardener Cecilio Rodríguez on what had previously been an immense rubbish heap, the Parque del Oeste was practically destroyed during the Civil War, when it provided a cover for the Republicans as the Nationalist troops invaded Madrid. Now rebuilt, it is one of the city's most appealing and romantic open spaces. The park contains birch, fir, atlas cedar and cypress trees, among others, as well as a 17,000sq m (183,000sq ft) rose garden, La Rosaleda, which hosts a rose festival each May. The *teleférico* (cable car) in the park runs out to the Casa de Campo, affording bird's-eye views over the west of Madrid. In summer, elegant, noisy terrace bars are set up along the Paseo de Pintor Rosales, Ernest Hemingway's favorite street.

Templo de Debod One of Madrid's most interesting attractions is not Spanish at all. The Debod Temple, at the park's southern corner, is a 4th-century BC Egyptian temple honoring the god Amon. It was installed in 1970 as a gift from the Egyptian government to Spanish engineers and archaeologists who had saved many treasures before large areas of land were flooded after the completion of the Aswan Dam.

Plaza de Oriente

Statues in the Plaza de Oriente, including an equestrian statue of Philip IV (middle)

Have an *aperitivo* on the terrace of the Café de Oriente, with the harmonious formal gardens stretching away in front of you to the Royal Palace. This is the place to reflect on the might of the monarchy at the height of its powers.

Ambitious emperor The elegant Plaza de Oriente was planned in 1811 under Joseph Bonaparte. To build it, he had to destroy the monuments and churches that then surrounded the Royal Palace. His original aim had been to build a kind of Champs-Élysées, running from the Plaza to the Cibeles Fountain. Fortunately, the Champs-Élysées project was abandoned; had it not been, Madrid would have lost, among many other treasures, the Monasterio de las Descalzas Reales (▷ 50; Convent of the Royal Shoeless Nuns). The existing square dates from the reign of Queen Isabella II (1830–1904). The attractively laid-out gardens contain statues of the kings and queens of Spain, which were originally intended for the top of the Royal Palace facing on to the plaza. They were never put into place because they were too heavy, and Isabella II dreamed that an earthquake made them topple over onto her.

Teatro Real At the eastern end of the square stands the Royal Theater, built between 1818 and 1850 and now restored. The open-air building that originally occupied the site was expanded in 1737 for a visit by Farinelli, the legendary castrato singer, of whom Philip V (1683–1746) was particularly fond.

THE BASICS

- E7
- Plaza de Oriente
- Café de Oriente
- Ópera
- 25

HIGHLIGHT

● The equestrian statue in the middle of the square of Philip IV by Montañes, taken from a portrait by Velázquez

PALACIO AND THE WEST TOP 25

More to See

BASILICA DE SAN FRANCISCO EL GRANDE

Built between 1761 and 1784, this church has a neoclassical facade by Francisco Sabatini, one of the greatest practitioners of this style, and an overwhelming 33m (108ft) dome by Miguel Fernández. The monastery was used as a barracks from 1835, after which it was lavishly redecorated. The interior (note the ceiling frescoes) contains much work by Spanish masters, including an early Goya, *The Sermon of San Bernadino de Siena,* in the first chapel on the left. There is also a museum.

➕ E8 ✉ Plaza de San Francisco, Calle de San Buenaventura 1 ☎ 91 365 38 00 🕐 Sep–Jul Tue–Fri 11–12.30, 4–6.30, Sat 11–1.30; Aug Tue–Sun 11–12.30, 5–7.30 🚇 La Latina 🚌 3, 60, 148 ♿ None 💵 Inexpensive

CENTRO CULTURAL CONDE DUQUE

Madrid's municipal art center is housed in an enormous 18th-century army barracks with a baroque facade. It includes a library, an auditorium and exhibition spaces but the principal attraction is the city's Museum of Contemporary Art, taking up two floors. Opened in 2001, the collection of 200 works by 177 artists is intended to complement, not compete with, Madrid's other art collections.

➕ E5 ✉ Conde Duque 9/11 ☎ 91 480 04 01 🚇 Plaza de España, Noviciado 🚌 1, 2, 21, 44, 74, 133 💵 Free

ESTACIÓN DE PRÍNCIPE PÍO

www.renfe.com

Restored and modernized, what was once the important Estación del Norte (North Station) is both a busy commuter railway station for the suburbs and a lively destination shopping complex (▷ 39), with cinemas in the Centro de Ocio (leisure center). There is also an important bus station outside what is still a handsome building, dating from the late 19th century. The station takes its name from Príncipe Pío, the nearby hill, where Spanish rebels were shot by French soldiers on 3 May 1808.

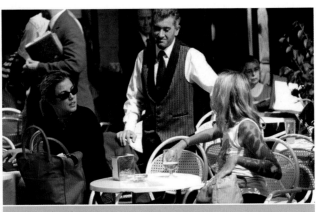

A café on Plaza de España

🕂 D6 ✉ Paseo de la Florida, corner of Cuesta de San Vicente 🚇 Metro Príncipe Pío 🚌 25, 33, 39, 41, 46, 75, 138

JARDINES DE LAS VISTILLAS

This park has wonderful views over the Casa de Campo toward the Guadarrama Mountains. A pleasant place for a relaxing drink.

🕂 D8 ✉ Travesia Vistillas 🚇 Ópera, La Latina 🚌 3, 148

MURALLA ARABE

What little we can see of the Arab Wall is the oldest surviving part of Madrid. It was originally part of the walls of the small Arab town of Magerit. The area around it, now the Parque Emir Mohammed I, is one of the venues for the popular autumn arts festival.

🕂 D8 ✉ Cuesta de la Vega 🚇 Ópera 🚌 3, 41, 148

PLAZA DE ESPAÑA

A statue of Cervantes stands at the western end of this grandiose square, overlooking a rather lovable 1815 statue of his two legendary creations, Don Quixote and Sancho Panza.

On the edge of the square, with a neo-baroque doorway, is the Edificio España, Madrid's first true skyscraper, while the 137m (450ft) Torre Madrid was a symbol of post-Civil War economic recovery and Europe's tallest building when it was built in 1957.

🕂 E6 ✉ Plaza de España 🚇 Plaza de España 🚌 68, 69, 74, 133

SAN NICOLÁS DE LOS SERVITAS

This is Madrid's oldest church and though much restored after the Civil War, its tower is evidence of the city's Arabic past. Designated a National Monument, the tower is probably the minaret of a mosque later consecrated as a Catholic church. This 12th-century tower is Mudéjar (built by Muslims under Christian rule), while the central apse is Gothic.

🕂 E7 ✉ Plaza de San Nicolás 6 ☎ 91 548 83 14 🕐 Mon 8.30–2, Sun 10–2, 6.30–8.30; do not visit during Mass. Not always open; advance phone call advisable 🚇 Ópera, La Latina

Plaza de España

A Walk West from Sol

Stroll through some of Madrid's oldest streets and squares; take in the grandeur of the Palace and gardens.

DISTANCE: 5km (3 miles) **ALLOW:** 2–3 hours

START

PUERTA DEL SOL
➕ F7 🚇 Puerta del Sol

END

ARGÜELLES
➕ D5 🚇 Argüelles

① Leave the Puerta del Sol at the western end and take Calle de Postas up to Plaza Mayor. Cross the plaza and exit at the diagonally opposite corner (El Arco de los Cuchilleros).

⑦ Follow the path around to the right and continue up to the Teleférico. Take a ride for fantastic views or cross Paseo Pintor Rasales and walk up Calle de Marqués Urquijo to Argüelles Metro station.

② At the bottom of the steps cross the street and go down Calle del Maestro de la Villa and into the Plaza Conde de Barajas.

⑥ Bear left, following the broad pavement to steps leading up the mound to the Templo de Debod. Walk past the temple to admire the views, descend the steps and turn right for the bandstand. Look down the hill to the Rosaleda rose garden.

③ Cross the square, turn right on Calle del Conde Miranda, right again on Calle del Codo and into the Plaza de la Villa.

④ Cross Calle Mayor and follow Calle de los Señores de Luzon to the Plaza de Ramales. Cross the square and go downhill to Calle de Lepanto, which leads to the Plaza de Oriente.

⑤ Turn left and walk past the statues to the Palacio Real. Turn right and follow the promenade, walking along the Sabatini Gardens. Do not go down into the tunnel, but climb the steps on the left and continue across the bottom of the Plaza de España.

Shopping

BERBERÍA DEL SAHARA Y EL SAHEL
The name of this shop is a clue: come here for unusual and authentic materials and crafts from North Africa and the Sahara region. What makes it different is space devoted to exhibitions, travel guides and other information on the region.
🏛 E8 ✉ Redondilla 8
☎ 91 354 01 76
🚇 La Latina

CENTRO COMERCIAL PRÍNCIPE PÍO
www.principepio.com
This conversion of a railway station (the 1881 Estacíon del Norte) is a fine example of the imaginative recycling of old buildings that is going on in Madrid. Not far from the Royal Palace and the Catedral de la Almudena, find fashion in the basement and restaurants on the ground floor, as well as cinemas.
🏛 D6 ✉ Paseo de la Florida ☎ 91 758 00 40
🚇 Príncipe Pío

Some outstanding Spanish stores in this shopping complex include:

LURUEÑA
www.luruena.es
Leather in all shapes and sizes, from shoes and bags, to sandals and high heels. Men can find a full range, from formal office wear to casual vacation shoes; women have a wider choice, with jazzy party bags and purses.
☎ 91 542 04 79

MASSIMO DUTTI WOMAN
www.massimodutti.com
This is an international Spanish company, despite its Italian name. Known for its classy style at mid-range prices, this store is devoted to women's clothing, as well as fragrances.
☎ 91 541 08 07

MUSEO DEL TRAJE
The Museo del Traje (▷ 31) has one of the best gift shops in the city. It sells a variety of goods with special emphasis on clothing, from delicate Spanish mantillas to elegant silk ties, plus a wonderful jewelry selection.
🏛 C3 ✉ 2 Avenida Juan

SHOES

Thanks to its centuries-old leather industry, Spain has long had a love affair with *zapatos* (shoes). Many of the world's leading designers are Spanish, mainly from Alicante, Valencia and the Balearic Islands. They range from the extremely expensive (Loewe) to the extremely popular (Camper). And the choice for men's and children's shoes is almost as wide as for women's. Known for its outlet shops with bargain prices is Calle de Augusto Figueroa in Chueca.

---

de Herrera ☎ 91 550 47 00 🚇 Moncloa, Ciudad Universitaria

PULL & BEAR
www.pullbear.com
Appealing to the young market, this is another great Spanish fashion industry success story. Both sexes are catered to and the clothes are sold at good prices.
☎ 91 542 06 91

TINO GONZÁLEZ
www.tinogonzalez.com
For imaginative yet practical shoes for men, women and children, Tino González has a wide range on offer, from formal to informal—and that special party pair.
☎ 91 632 44 90

TONI MARTIN
www.tonimartindiscos.com
This music shop, which specializes in country, jazz and rock 'n' roll, stocks a great selection of CDs and vinyl, new and second-hand.
🏛 E6 ✉ Calle Martin de los Heros 18 ☎ 91 542 50 20
🚇 Plaza de España 🚌 1, 2, 44, 74, 183

TRUCCO
www.trucco.es
Rather than fashionistas, Trucco appeals to women with flair, who value attention to detail and quality. This is another popular and reliable Spanish-made international fashion franchise.
☎ 91 484 44 00

Entertainment and Nightlife

COPÉRNICO NOVA CLUB

www.salacopernico.es
Close to the university campus, this is the place to hear live bands from every part of the spectrum, from punk to metal. The decor is themed on a galleon, with telescopes and globes. Reasonable door charges.

➕ E4 ✉ Calle Fernández de los Ríos 67 ☎ 91 562 62 56 🕔 Nightly 11pm–6am 🚇 Moncloa

CORRAL DE LA MORERÍA

www.corraldelamoreria.com
A legendary flamenco *tablao*-restaurant which has been going strong for over 50 years. Open daily from 8pm, with two shows, each lasting an hour and a half, starting at 10pm and midnight. Reservation advised.

➕ E8 ✉ Calle de la Morería 17 ☎ 91 365 8446 🚇 Opera

ELANUET

For anyone who loves 80s music, head here for techno pop.

➕ E8 ✉ Calle Segovia 24 ☎ No phone 🕔 Wed–Sun 11pm–3.30am 🚇 La Latina

GOLEM CINE

www.golem.es
Originally an art house cinema, Golem still shows international films in original versions with Spanish subtitles. The movie theater also has a good basement café.

➕ E6 ✉ Calle Martin de los Heros 14 ☎ 91 559 38 36 🕔 Check for times 🚇 Plaza de España

EL LIMBO

Showing clips from films projected onto big screens, live bands and DJs, this is a popular venue with teenagers on a fun night out.

➕ E8 ✉ Calle Bailén 39 ☎ 91 365 21 58 🕔 Mon–Sat 10pm–3.30am 🚇 La Latina

MARULA CAFÉ

www.marulacafe.com
Soulfood sessions, funk and more at this popular club with live DJs. Cool bar, and an outdoor terrace in summer.

➕ E8 ✉ Calle Caños Viejos 3 ☎ 91 366 15 96 🕔 Mon–Sat 11pm–6am 🚇 La Latina

---

BOOM INDUSTRY

There are at least 60 cinemas in Madrid. Most have a discount day (Monday or Wednesday), when tickets are half price. Always arrive well in advance for evening weekend showings; queues can start forming an hour before projection time. Bigger cinemas now have advanced reservations and most have reserved seating on weekends. Movie information is published in full in all the daily newspapers: earliest showings (*pasos*) are generally at 4, latest at 10.30.

PRINCESA

www.cinesrenoir.com
Since it opened in the mid 1990s, this has become the city's main screening point for new Spanish films.

➕ E6 ✉ Calle Princesa 3 ☎ 91 542 27 02 🚇 Plaza de España

RENOIR

www.cinesrenoir.com
The best of the cinemas clustered around the bottom of Calle Martín de los Heros, near the Plaza de España, shows the latest art films. Detailed information sheets are published (in Spanish) to accompany each one. There are late showings on weekends.

➕ E6 ✉ Calle Martín de los Heros 12 ☎ 91 542 27 02 🚇 Plaza de España

STAR CAFÉ

Bands from Europe and the US perform rock and blues live Wed–Sat in this American-style café-bar, which serves hamburgers and french fries, ribs and pasta dishes. There is a good choice of beers and cocktails.

➕ D/E5 ✉ Calle Serrano Jovér 5 ☎ 91 542 28 17 🚇 Argüelles

TEATRO REAL

www.teatro-real.com
The grandest and most beautiful of the European opera houses.

➕ E7 ✉ Plaza de Isabel II ☎ 91 516 06 60/902 24 48 🚇 Ópera

Restaurants

PRICES

Prices are approximate, based on a 3-course meal for one person.

€€€	over €50
€€	€30–€50
€	under €30

A'CASIÑA (€€)

The Columnas, just one of the restaurant's large dining areas, is a sunlit indoor terrace overlooking the park. Start with *arroz caldoso con bogavante*, a rich lobster soup cooked with rice, and follow up with the hake (*merluza*). Reservations are essential at this restaurant.

🚩 B7/8 ✉ Avenida de Angel, Casa de Campo ☎ 91 526 34 25 🕒 Closed Sun night 🚇 Lago

LA BOLA TABERNA (€€)

www.labola.es
La Bola has been in business for 100 years. It's best known for its *cocido madrileño* (a soup-style stew with noodles, chickpeas, meat and vegetables), presented in a sizzling pot. No credit cards.

🚩 E7 ✉ Calle de la Bola 5 ☎ 91 547 69 30 🕒 Closed Sun night 🚇 Ópera, Santo Domingo

CAFÉ DE ORIENTE (€€€)

www.cafedeoriente.es
Built on the remains of a convent and facing the Royal Palace, this is a rather aristocratic place, with distinctive dishes that fuse *madrileño* with French cuisine.

🚩 E7 ✉ Plaza de Oriente 2 ☎ 91 541 39 74 🚇 Ópera

CASA MINGO (€)

www.casamingo.es
A popular Asturian *sidrería* or cider house. The idea is to pour the cider into the glass from a great height and drink it very fast. The best tapas here are based on the strong Cabrales cheese.

🚩 C6 ✉ Paseo de la Florida 34 ☎ 91 547 79 18 🚇 Príncipe Pío

DANTXARI (€€–€€€)

www.dantxari.com
This Basque tavern offers spicy cod, and lamb with garlic and wild mush-

REGIONAL CUISINE

Spanish regional cusine—particularly that of the Basque country—has achieved greater international recognition than the cuisine of Madrid itself. Basque and Catalan cuisine tends to be fish-based, though if you do order meat, it is likely to come in the form of a huge steak. Basque tapas are available at some of the Basque restaurants; these are little culinary works of art. Galician specialties include seafood and hearty peasant dishes. The Asturians are known for their cider and *fabadas*, bean-based stews.

rooms. There is a wide-ranging Spanish wine list and the service is cheerful.

🚩 E6 ✉ Ventura Rodriguez 8 ☎ 91 542 35 24 🕒 Lunch, dinner. Closed Sun, public hols 🚇 Ventura Rodríguez

EL INGENIO (€€)

www.restauranteingenio.com
This restaurant, close to Plaza Santo Domingo, serves traditional Spanish cuisine. You'll find salads, croquettes, wild mushrooms with aioli, vegetable stew, dried butterbean dishes and fresh cod on the menu. The place has a literary feel—Don Quixote para-phernalia adorn the walls. Reserving in advance is advisable, as it's a very popular place.

🚩 E6 ✉ Calle de Leganitos 10 ☎ 91 541 91 33 🕒 Closed Sun, public hols 🚇 Santo Domingo

LAZEMA (€€–€€€)

With its cool modern interior and summer terrace, the restaurant in the Museo del Traje has to be one of the best places in a museum in the world to eat. Roberto Hierro and his team prepare stunning Basque cuisine. For a real treat try the Saturday tasting menu to experience the full range of specialties.

🚩 C3 ✉ Avenida de Juan de Herrera 2 ☎ 91 550 20 55 🕒 Closed Sun, Mon 🚇 Ciudad Universitaria, Moncloa

MESÓN CINCO JOTAS (€€)

www.mesoncincojotas.com
One of a chain of well-run Cinco Jotas (5 Js) that pride themselves on serving the best quality (5 star, or 5 J) Iberian ham from Jabugo. Choose between the restaurant and the tapas bar.
🔳 E3 ✉ Calle Arenal 6 ☎ 91 522 78 48 🕐 Daily 12.30–midnight, weekends till 1am 🚇 Ópera

EL MOLINO DE LOS PORCHES (€€€)

Join throngs of locals who come here for old-fashioned *asado*, the roast meat that is both the house specialty and a Castilian specialty. Book early, especially in summer.
🔳 D5 ✉ Paseo Pintor Rosales 1 ☎ 91 548 13 36 🕐 Daily noon–midnight 🚇 Argüelles

PRADA A TOPE (€€)

Rustic and comfortable, this tavern is enhanced with aged-wood fittings. The cuisine is from León, which is known for its smoked beef, and this restaurant does it proud. *Cocido*, *tortilla*, roast beef and spicy green peppers are all on the menu. Two branches in Madrid.
🔳 D7 ✉ Cuesta de San Vicente 32 ☎ 91 559 39 53 🕐 Closed Tue 🚇 Plaza de España, Príncipe Pío
Also: 🔳 G7 ✉ Príncipe 11 ☎ 91 429 59 21 🕐 Closed Sun dinner, Mon 🚇 Sevilla

SAL GORDA (€€)

www.restaurantsalgorda.es
This long-established restaurant is off the beaten tourist trail and is very popular with locals for its dishes: Spanish through and through. This restaurant is a good choice and gives excellent value for money.
🔳 E2 ✉ Beatriz de Bobadilla 9 ☎ 91 553 95 06 🕐 Closed Sun, Aug 🚇 Guzmán el Bueno

SANLÚCAR (€)

Sanlúcar is a classic Andalucian-style tapas bar with owners from Cadiz, so a range of sherries are the perfect accompaniment for dishes laden with prawns, *langostinos* (crayfish) and a variety of other seafood. Try the well-priced three-course menu of the day.
🔳 E8 ✉ San Isidro Labrador 14 ☎ 91 354 00 52 🕐 Closed Sun dinner, Mon 🚇 La Latina

REGIONAL FARE

After the Basques, the Galicians have the best cuisine in Spain. Together with their neighbors the Asturians, they prefer maritime cuisine, and portions are generally sizeable, with potatoes the staple food. Regional special dishes include *pulpo* (octopus), and *pimientos de Padrón* (hot green peppers)—best eaten with a jug of water.

EL SENADOR (€€)

www.restaurantesenador.com
This well-established traditional restaurant serves Segovian cuisine. The house special is roast lamb, but there are also steaks cooked on a charcoal fire and fresh fish. The wine is great, and so are the desserts. Tapas are available at the bar. Reserve in advance.
🔳 E7 ✉ Plaza de la Marina Española 2 ☎ 91 541 22 21 🕐 Closed Sun night 🚇 Santo Domingo, Ópera

TABERNA DEL ALABARDERO (€€€)

www.grupolezama.es
A plush restaurant next to the Teatro Real named after the soldiers of the king's bodyguard. You're likely to rub shoulders with politicians, bullfighters and literary figures here. If you can't afford the price of a meal you can still have excellent tapas at one of the bar's terrace tables.
🔳 E7 ✉ Felipe V 6 ☎ 91 547 25 77 🕐 Daily 🚇 Ópera

LA TAQUERÍA DE BIRRA (€)

www.lastaquerias.com
Where locals come to get their fill of Mexican dishes, such as tacos (including vegetarian tacos). Jolly atmosphere, with Mexican music.
🔳 E8 ✉ Don Pedro 11 ☎ 91 366 45 39 🕐 Daily 7.30–2.30am; weekends, public hols 1pm–2.30am 🚇 Ópera

This is the Madrid that most visitors expect to see: medieval lanes, great art museums, and tapas bars on every corner. It's best explored on foot.

5

6

7

8

9

San Martín
Calle de Desengañ

GRAN VÍA

Gran Vía **GRAN** VÍ
Plaza de
Callao
Callao
Plaza de
Carmer
Monasterio
de las Descalzas
Reales
Calle
Calle del
Arenal
Sol

Plaza de
San Martín
Calle
Mayor
MAYOR
Plaza de
San Ginés
Puerta
del Sol

Plaza
Pontejos
Plaza de
Carretas

Plaza de
la Villa
CALLE
Catedral las
Carboneras
Plaza
San Miguel
Arco de los
Cuchilleros
Plaza
Mayor
Plaza de Bolsa
Calle de Bolsa
Plaza
Jacinto
Benavente

Ayuntamiento
Calle de
Sacramento
Artzobispal
Castrense
San Pedro
el Viejo
Plaza del
Conde de
Barajas
Palacio de
San Cruz
San
Cruz
CENTRO

Plaza de
la Paja
Calle del Nuño
Puerta
Cerrada
Calle concepción Jerónima
Colegiata de
San Isidro
Tirso de
Molina

San
Andres
Plaza
San Andres
Plaza
Humilladero
Cra. S Franc la Cebada
Calle Don Pedro
Plaza de
la Cebada
Plaza Tirso
de Molina
Calle D Alba
Call

Plaza de
Mercado
La Latina
Plaza de
Cascorro
Calle de Juanelo
San Millán y
San Cayetano

GRAN VÍA DE SAN FRANCISCO
Calle de Calatrava
Plaza
General
Vara de Rey
Plaza
Santa Ana
Calle del
Mesón de
Paredes

V de la
Paloma
Calle Carlos Arniches
Calle de Rodas
El Rastro
San
Fernando

RONDA DE SEGOVIA
Puerta de
Toledo
Glorieta
Puerta de
Toledo
RONDA
DE
TOLEDO
EMBAJADORES
Casino
de la Reina
Glorieta d
Embajadores

Calle Concejal Benito Martín Loranzo

0   250 m
0   250 yds

D   **E**   **F**

The museum's glass elevators (opposite, below left and right); Picasso's Guernica (middle)

Museo Nacion...
Reina Sofía

In Madrid's leading modern art museum, the home of Picasso's *Guernica*, you might not like all the works on display. But even on its busiest days, the light and airy space is a delight.

A triumph of planning Inspired by the Pompidou Center in Paris, this 12,540sq m (135,000sq ft) space is Madrid's finest contemporary art museum; among European museums only the Pompidou is larger. It occupies a building that served as the San Carlos hospital between 1977 and 1986. Transparent elevators on the outside whisk you up for a thrilling view over the rooftops of Madrid. The fine permanent collection showcases Spanish art of the 20th century—cubism, surrealism, realism, informalism. The dramatic extension by French architect Jean Nouvel opened in 2004. Under the red roof are galleries for temporary exhibitions, as well as the library, shop, café and auditorium.

Guernica Picasso's masterpiece dominates the Reina Sofía. When it was commissioned by the Republican Government for display at the 1937 Paris Exhibition, the only instruction was that it be big: it measures 6.4 by 7m (21 by 23ft). Taking his inspiration from the Nationalist bombing of the Basque town of Guernica in 1937, this painting has become 20th-century art's great anti-war symbol. Many saw the 1995 decision to remove the bullet-proof screen that had protected it for many years as a symbolic gesture, showing that democracy in Spain had finally taken root.

THE BASICS

www.museoreinasofia.es

✚ G9

✉ Calle Santa Isabel 52

☎ 91 774 10 00

🕐 Mon, Wed–Sat 10–9, Sun 10–2.30

🍴 Bar, restaurant

🚇 Atocha

🚆 Atocha

🚌 6, 10, 14, 24, 26, 27, 32, 34, 36, 37, 41, 45, 47, 55, 57, 85, 86

♿ Very good

💶 Moderate. Free to under 18s, over 65s; Sat afternoon and Sun

HIGHLIGHTS

● View from exterior elevators
● Enclosed patio
● *Guernica*, Picasso
● Joan Gris Room
● Picasso Room
● Joan Miró Room
● Dalí Room
● Surrealism Room
● Luis Buñuel Room
● Spanish 20th-Century Art Room

Museo Thyssen-Bornemisza

HIGHLIGHTS

● *Portrait of Giovanna Tornabuoni*, Domenico Ghirlandaio
● *Portrait of Henry VIII*, Holbein
● *St. Catherine of Alexandria*, Caravaggio
● *Annunciation Diptych*, Van Eyck
● *St. Jerome in the Wilderness*, Titian
● *The Lock*, Constable
● *Easter Morning*, Caspar David Friedrich
● *Les Vessenots*, Van Gogh
● *Man with a Clarinet*, Picasso

TIP

● In summer, the rooftop terrace is open for romantic dinners. Also in summer, the museum is open late at night.

This is one of the best things that has happened to Madrid since the end of the Civil War. It is also one of the few internationally renowned art museums where everything is priority viewing.

New museum The collection was begun by the German financier and industrialist Baron Heinrich Thyssen-Bornemisza in the 1920s and continued after his death by his son, Hans Heinrich (who died in 2002). The 775 paintings exhibited here were sold to the Spanish state for a mere $350 million in 1993, one year after the museum opened to the public. The permanent collection, spanning seven centuries, is housed in the sympathetically renovated 18th-century Palacio de Villahermosa. In 2004, the glass pavilion opened. It contains 19th- and 20th-century paintings from the collection of Hans Heinrich's widow, Carmen Thyssen-Bornemisza, a former Miss Spain.

The collection The sheer variety of the many works on display prompted some to call the Thyssen over-eclectic; others claim its very quirkiness is part of its charm. Each room highlights a different period: the top floor is devoted to art from medieval times through to the 17th century; the second floor to rococo and neoclassicism of the 18th and 19th centuries through to fauvism and expressionism; the first level to 20th-century surrealism, pop art and the avant-garde. Start from the top and work your way down. It is worth renting an audio guide, available in Spanish, English, French, German and Italian. The museum's shop is one of the best, whether you are looking for art books or beautiful gifts.

THE BASICS

www.museothyssen.org

✚ G7

✉ Paseo del Prado 8

☎ 902 76 05 11

🕐 Tue–Sun 10–7, Mon 12–4

🍽 Café, restaurant

🚆 Atocha, Recoletos

Ⓜ Banco de España

🚌 1, 2, 5, 9, 10, 14, 15, 20, 27, 34, 37, 45, 51, 52, 53, 74, 146, 150

♿ Excellent ❓ Bookstore

💵 Expensive. Free to children under 12; reduction to over 65s. Free Mon 12–4

Monasterio de las Descalzas Reales

Marble tomb of the
Empress Maria (left)
at the Monasterio de
las Descalzas Reales
(right)

THE BASICS

www.patrimonionacional.es

🚼 F7

✉ Plaza de las Descalzas
Reales 3

☎ 91 454 88 00

🕐 Tue–Sat 10–2, 4–6.30,
Sun and public hols 10–3

🚇 Sol, Ópera

🚌 3, 25, 39, 148

♿ None

💵 Moderate

HIGHLIGHTS

● *Recumbent Christ*, Gaspar
Becerra
● *Neapolitan Nativity*
(Chapel of St. Michael)
● *Bust of the Mater
Dolorosa*, José Risueño
● *Cardinal Infante Don
Fernando of Austria*, Rubens
● *The Ship of the Church*,
16th-century painting
● *Adoration of the Magi*,
Brueghel
● *The Empress María*, Goya
● 17th-century tapestries

Though the tour of the Royal Shoeless Nuns' Convent is conducted at a brisk pace, the building contains an unusually high proportion of unmissable treasures.

Convent history Of Madrid's two monastery museums, the Descalzas Reales is the richer; most of its rooms are small museums in themselves. Founded by Juana of Austria, the younger daughter of Charles V, on the site of the place in which she was born, it was built between 1559 and 1564 in Madrid brick by Antonio Silla and Juan Bautista of Toledo. The whole place breathes mid-17th-century religious mysticism, though the 'vile stink' of which traveler William Beckford complained when attending Mass in the late 18th century has departed. The original sisters were all of noble or aristocratic blood, and each founded a chapel on reception into the order: there are 33 of them, and to this day the convent is home to 23 Franciscan nuns, each of whom maintains one of the chapels. The Grand Staircase, with its *trompe l'oeil* portrait of Philip IV and his family standing on the balcony, is covered with frescoes by the artist Claudio Coello. With its incongruous location right in the middle of commercial Madrid, it is a small miracle that it remains intact.

Seeing the collection The only way to see the convent is to take a tour. Given in Spanish only, it lasts around 45 minutes and is conducted at such a frenzied pace that it is worth buying a guide book at the entrance. The church can be visited only during Mass, at 8am or 7pm.

Plaza Mayor

The cobbled Plaza Mayor strikes a chord with everyone entering it for the first time: it's here that you fully realize you are in the capital of Spain.

Work in progress Built in the 15th century as a market square, and later renamed the Plaza del Arrabal (Square outside the Walls), the Plaza Mayor came into its own when Philip II, after making Madrid the capital of Spain, ordered it rebuilt as the administrative center of the Court. The only part to be completed immediately was the Panadería, or the bakery, by architect Diego Sillero in 1590 (the frescoes are the work of the early 1990s), while the rest of it was completed in 1619 by Juan Gómez de la Mora under Philip III, whose bronze statue stands in the middle. After a fire in 1790, much of the square had to be rebuilt. The buildings between the towers on either side are Town Hall offices; the rest are private homes. The 18th-century Arco de los Cuchilleros, leading from the square into Cava Baja, is named after the cutlers who once worked here making knives for local butchers and swords for the nobility.

A gathering place The Plaza Mayor was where the more important members of the Court lived during the 17th century; at the end of the century, the square became the site of mounted bullfights, carnivals and the terrible *autos da fé* of the Spanish Inquisition, attended by thousands on 30 June 1680, when 118 offenders were executed in a single day. Hangings were also carried out here until the end of the 18th century.

THE BASICS

➕ F7/8
✉ Plaza Mayor
🍴 *Terraza* bars around square
Ⓜ Sol, Ópera
🚌 3, 17, 18, 23, 31, 35
❓ Tourist office in square

TIPS

● In May, free concerts are held during the 2 May and San Isidro festivities.
● The plaza hosts the city's annual Christmas market.

CENTRO TOP 25

51

Puerta del Sol

TOP **25**

The bear and tree, symbol of Madrid (left); statue of Carlos III (middle and right)

THE BASICS

⊞ F7
✉ Puerta del Sol
Ⓢ Sol
🚌 3, 5, 15, 20, 51, 52, 150

HIGHLIGHTS

● Bear and *madroño* (strawberry tree) statue
● Statue of Charles III
● La Mallorquina pastry shop
● Newspaper stands: a major part of Madrid streetlife
● Tio Pepe sign
● Kilometer Zero
● Doña Manolita's lottery ticket kiosk

Almost inevitably, you will cross this square several times. For many *madrileños*, it is the true soul of the city and each year thousands gather here to see in the New Year.

Soul of Madrid The area's namesake gateway was demolished in 1570 when the square was widened to receive Anne of Austria, Philip II's fourth wife. The design of the present square dates back to 1861; the building on the south side, the Casa de Correos, is from 1768. Originally the Post Office, it is now the headquarters of the Madrid regional government. Spain's Kilometer Zero, the point from which all distances in Spain are measured, can be found on the pavement in front of it. The clock and tower were built in 1867.

A troubled past The Esquilache mutiny of 1766 began here, sparked by Charles III's uncharacteristically tyrannical insistence that the population should wear short capes and three-cornered hats to emulate a hated French style. The most notable moment in Sol's history was on 2 and 3 May 1808, when *madrileños* took up arms against occupying French troops, a heroic resistance in which more than 2,000 died, immortalized in Goya's two magnificent anti-war paintings in the Prado, *Dos de Mayo* and *Tres de Mayo*. It was here, also, that politician José Canalejas was assassinated in 1912, and the Second Republic was proclaimed in 1931. It remains a popular meeting place, especially by the monument of the bear with a strawberry tree, the symbol of Madrid.

El Rastro

THE BASICS

www.elrastro.org
🔳 F9
✉ Ribera de Curtidores
🕐 8–2.30
🍴 Many cafés and bars
🚇 Tirso de Molina

HIGHLIGHTS

● Street vendors shouting
● Spanish pottery
● Antiques at Galerías Piquer
● Leather boots and saddles
at Curtidos Roman, Calle
Ribera de Curtidores 16

For locals and visitors alike, this is the classic place to spend a leisurely Sunday morning. The Rastro is much more than a flea market; crowds bustle as if they are off to a football match. Be careful with your valuables.

Bargains galore Start from the Tirso de Molina Metro station, and head for the Plaza de Cascorro. The lines of stalls run downhill, along both sides and in the middle of the Ribera de Curtidores street, and go on to form a busy triangle with Calle de Toledo and Calle Embajadores. It all gets underway at 9am, and the trick is to take your time and to tuck all your valuables away. Bargains are here for those who poke, prod and haggle for old birdcages and cheap underwear, leather bags and clay pots.

A bloody history But the shopping experience is not limited to just the main street. All the regular shops are open, and the market spills into the side streets. Find pets on Calle de Fray Ceferino González, and every sort of painting, from watercolors and prints to original oils, on the Calle de San Cayetano, nicknamed the Painters' Street. Drop by the Galerías Piquér (▷ 62), a courtyard surrounded by antiques shops. As for the name, *rastro* dates back to the 16th century, when this was the site of a slaughterhouse. When the dead animals were dragged away to the tanners (*curtidores*), they left a *rastro*, trail of blood on the street.

Real Academia de Bellas Artes

HIGHLIGHTS

● Goya self-portraits (Room 20)
● *The Burial of the Sardine*, Goya (Room 20)
● *Alonso Rodríguez*, Francisco Zurbarán (Room 6)
● *Head of John the Baptist*, José de Ribera (Room 3)
● *Felipe IV*, Velázquez (Room 11)
● *Susana and the Elders*, Rubens (Room 13)
● *Spring*, Giuseppe Arcimboldo (Room 14)
● Goya etchings (Calcografía Nacional)

TIP

● Don't miss the Calcografía Nacional, with its room dedicated to Goya's disturbing engravings.

The Prado, Thyssen and Reina Sofía may have more visitors, but the eclectic collections of the Royal Academy of Fine Arts, the oldest permanent art institution in Madrid, are interesting to see.

History It was Francisco Meléndez who suggested the establishment of a Royal Academy on the model of those in Rome, Paris, Florence and other great cities. Work began on the authorization of Philip V in 1744 and was completed under Fernando VI in 1752. The Academy was initially in the Casa de la Panadería, in the Plaza Mayor, but Charles III transferred it to its present site in 1773. The original building was baroque, but shortly after it opened, Academy members with conservative tastes insisted that it be given today's neoclassical facade. This museum is rarely

Alonso Rodríguez, *by Francisco Zurbarán, (left) on display at the Royal Academy of Fine Arts (right)*

overcrowded and it is small enough to be visited comfortably in a couple of hours.

Layout The museum has three floors. The best-known galleries are on the second floor, most notably Room 20, with its Goyas. Other highlights by 17th-century Spanish artists include *Head of John the Baptist* by José de Ribera (1591–1652), *Alonso Rodríguez* by Francisco Zurbarán, and *Felipé IV* by Velázquez. *Spring,* by the 16th-century Milanese painter Giuseppe Arcimboldo, in Room 14, is the only Arcimboldo in Spain and one of only a handful in the world. Halfway up the stairs to the entrance (and easily missed) is another museum, La Calcografía Nacional, or Engraving Plates Museum. The Gabinete Goya at the back of this contains a beautifully displayed series of the original plates used by the artist for his etchings.

THE BASICS

www.realacademiabella-sartessanfernando.com

➕ G7

✉ Calle de Alcalá 13

☎ 91 524 08 64

🕐 Tue–Sun 10–3

🚇 Sol, Sevilla

🚌 3, 5, 15, 20, 51, 52, 53, 150

♿ Limited

💶 Moderate. Free to under 18s, over 65s

More to See

CAIXAFORUM

www.obrasocial.lacaixa.es

This exhibition space and concert hall is an extraordinary piece of architecture. What was a power station now has an alien, upward extension sprouting from its roof and a deep porch, making it look as if the mass above is hovering above the ground. What would otherwise be an ugly bare wall in front of the entrance has been transformed into a 'vertical garden', a mass of dripping greenery.
🕇 H8 ✉ Paseo del Prado 36 ☎ 91 330 73 00 🕐 Daily 10–8 🚇 Atocha 🚌 10, 14, 27, 34, 45 ⛝ Free, occasional charge for certain concerts

CALLE MAYOR

This is perhaps the most traditional of Madrid's streets, with some old-fashioned shops—including a wonderful guitarrería (guitar store) near the Calle Bailén end. Spain's two greatest playwrights, Lope de Vega and Calderón de la Barca, lived at Nos. 25 and 61 respectively.
🕇 E/F7 🚇 Sol 🚌 3

CALLE DEL MESÓN DE PAREDES

To get a complete sense of the multicultural atmosphere of Madrid's *barrio popular*, stroll down this street and those around it on any weekday morning, when it is bustling and full of life. La Corrala is an 1882 example of the corridor-tenement found throughout work-ing-class Madrid. From the early 1980s, it was used for productions as an open-air theater. It is now an Artistic Monument. The Taberna de Antonio Sánchez at No. 13 (▷ 66) is one of the best-preserved examples of Madrid's traditional 19th-century bars, or *tabernas*. A few others survive around the old parts of the city, some of them still with their original tile work, marble-topped tables and polished zinc counters.
🕇 F9 🚇 Tirso de Molina, Lavapies 🚌 32, 57

CASA MUSEO LOPE DE VEGA

Spain's greatest playwright, Felix Lope de Vega (1562–1635), lived in this

Gran Vía

house from 1610 until his death. Now an evocative museum, the rooms are furnished in the style of the period, based on an inventory by Lope himself. There are lovely gardens behind this museum, which you will find just uphill from the Paseo.

🔶 G8 ✉ Calle de Cervantes 11 ☎ 91 429 92 16 🕐 Tue–Sun 10–3 🚇 Banco de España, Antón Martín 🚌 On Paseo del Prado 🎫 Free

COLEGIATA DE SAN ISIDRO

San Isidro is the patron saint of Madrid and, between 1885 and 1993, until the completion of the Almudena (▷ 25), this immense baroque church was Madrid's unofficial cathedral. Built in 1620 by Pedro Sánchez for the Jesuits, the church was commandeered by Charles III after he expelled them. San Isidro's remains, until then in San Andrés, were brought here at that time.

🔶 F8 ✉ Calle Colegiata 17 ☎ 91 369 20 37 🕐 Daily 7–1.30, 5–9 🚇 Tirso de Molina, La Latina 🚌 3, 6, 17, 18, 23, 26, 32, 50, 60, 148 🚫 None 🎫 Free

GRAN VÍA

Running between the Calle de Alcalá and the Plaza de España, the massive Gran Vía is one of the city's great axes; with its shops and cinemas, it is very lively and stimulating for early evening strolls. Begun in 1910 under Alfonso XII, it led to the shortening or destruction of 54 other streets. Serving as Madrid's great northern axis, the road peels off from Calle de Alcalá a short way from Plaza de Cibeles. It was conceived in the late 19th century as a way to allow Madrid to expand. Work finally began in 1910 and was completed in 1929. The building of this thoroughfare provided an opportunity for architects of the early 20th century to apply new styles. The best are at the start of the street, on or near the junction of Alcalá and the Gran Vía. The most striking building is the Edificio Metropolis, which was finished in 1911. Its slate dome is ornamented with gold and topped by a winged statue of Victory. Next to it is No. 1 Gran Vía, the Edificio Grassy (1917), named after the jeweler's shop in the

A portrait of Lope de Vega at his former home, Casa Museo Lope de Vega

ground floor and distinguished by its colonnaded tower. Moving up the street, on the north side (No. 12) is a 1931 art deco cocktail bar, Museo Chicote, made famous by its association with author Ernest Hemingway and the Hollywood actress Ava Gardner. Don't miss the Telefónica building (No. 28), a Manhattan-style skyscraper, the tallest building in Madrid when it was erected in 1929.

✚ F/G7 🚇 Gran Via, Callao 🚌 44, 46, 74, 133, 146, 147, 148, 149

PLAZA DEL CONDE DE BARAJAS

Looking for a special souvenir of Madrid? Visit this delightful spot on a Sunday, when artists set up their stalls to sell oil paintings and water-colors. Prices range from cheap to unbelievable, but it is worth haggling. At Christmas, concerts and flamenco dancing events are also held here. It's located southwest of the Plaza Mayor between Calle de la Pasa and the Pasadizo del Panecillo.

✚ E8 🚇 La Latina

PLAZA DE LAS CORTES

www.congreso.es

This is the home of the Congreso de los Diputados, or parliament build-ings. The ceremonial entrance to the parliament is guarded by two bronze lions popularly known as Daoíz and Velarde after the heroic captains of the Napoleonic invasion. An attempted military coup took place inside the building in 1981, and was recorded on video for posterity. There are weekly guided tours. In the middle of the square stands a statue of Spain's most famous author, Miguel de Cervantes (1547–1616), renowned for his novel *Don Quixote*.

✚ G7 ✉ Plaza de las Cortes 🚇 Sevilla 🚌 5, 150, N5, N6

PLAZA DE LA PAJA

During Muslim rule, this pleasant little Straw Square was the site of the city's most important *zoco*, or street market; during the Middle Ages it housed aristocratic residences. Of the many palaces located here, the most notable is at No. 14, the Lasso de

Congreso de los Diputados on Plaza de las Cortes

An outdoor café on Plaza de la Paja

Castilla, the preferred residence of Catholic kings when they stayed in Madrid, sadly now extremely unpalatial in appearance.

⊞ E8 ⊠ Plaza de la Paja 🚇 La Latina 🚌 3, 31, 148

PLAZA DE SANTA ANA

Once occupied by the Santa Ana monastery, which was torn down during Joseph Bonaparte's rule (1808–13), the refurbished plaza is surrounded by bars and is perfect for people-watching in summer. The square is home to the oldest theater in Madrid, Teatro Español, which was built in 1745 and puts on classical Spanish productions.

⊞ F8 ⊠ Plaza de Santa Ana 🚇 Sol, Sevilla 🚌 5, 150

PLAZA DE LA VILLA

With its small scale, this rectangular and typically Castilian square makes a pleasant change from some of the more imposing buildings in Madrid. Originally the site of an Arab street market, it is now home to three buildings in three distinct styles: the Castilian-baroque Ayuntamiento, the Casa de la Villa, designed in 1630 by Juan Gómez de Mora; the much-restored Casa de Cisneros, on the south side of the square, one of Madrid's finest examples of the plateresque style prevalent in the 16th century; and the Torre de los Lujanes, one of the city's few surviving monuments from the 15th century.

⊞ E8 ⊠ Plaza de la Villa 🚇 Sol, Ópera 🚌 3

SAN PEDRO EL VIEJO

Noteworthy principally for its 14th-century Mudéjar tower and the legends surrounding it, San Pedro stands on the site of an old mosque. In the doorway are the only coats of arms extant from the period preceding the Catholic monarchs. Part of the interior dates from the 15th century, while the rest is largely of 18th-century construction.

⊞ E8 ⊠ Calle Nuncio 14 ☎ 91 365 12 84 🕐 Daily 6–8pm; do not visit during Mass 🚇 La Latina, Tirso de Molina ♿ None

Casa de Guadalajara on Plaza de Santa Ana

A Walk East from Sol

Take this walk to see the Spanish parliament and the Prado, the Botanic Gardens and Retiro Park.

DISTANCE: 6.7km (4 miles) **ALLOW:** 2–3 hours

START

PUERTA DEL SOL
➕ F7 🚇 Puerta del Sol

1 Start on the Puerta del Sol. Exit at its eastern end and walk down Calle de San Jerónimo, all the way to the Plaza de las Cortes. Continue past the south side of the Museo Thyssen-Bornemisza to the Plaza de Cánovas de Castillo.

2 Turn right down the Paseo del Prado and cross at Plaza de la Platería de Martínez. Visit the Jardín Botánico, on the south side of the Prado. Or continue along Calle de Espalter to Calle de Moreto.

3 Turn left and walk uphill, past San Jerónimo del Real, to Calle de Félipe IV. Turn right, walk up past the Casón del Buen Retiro, cross Calle de Alfonso XII and enter the Retiro Park.

END

CALLE DE ALCALÁ
➕ G7 🚇 Banco de España

7 Continue past the Plaza de las Silesa and turn sharp left down Calle de Barquillo. Follow this all the way down to Calle de Alcalá.

6 At the Plaza de Colón, turn left on Paseo de Recoletos. Cross over at the entrance to Recoletos station. On the west side of the Paseo, turn right on Calle Bárbara de Braganza.

5 At the fountain, bear left for the Puerta de Alcalá, cross Calle de Alcalá, and walk up Calle de Serrano. Pass the Archaeological Museum and turn left on Calle de Jorge Juan.

4 Stroll through the parterre gardens and up the steps at the end. When you reach the lake, turn left and follow its edge. Across the water you will see the dramatic Alfonso XII monument.

AMPARO MERCERÍA

As this grand old haberdashery store confirms, stitching and mending, sewing and knitting are still popular skills in Spain. Founded back in 1861, the store retains that sense of history with a solid wooden counter, as well as selections of buttons, needles, sequins and lace.

✛ F7 ✉ Calle Marqués Viudo de Pontejos 5 ☎ 91 521 98 08 🚇 Sol

ANTIGUA CASA TALAVERA

For fine hand-painted ceramics from Talavera, Granada and Toledo. This 100-year-old establishment has both original and reproduction vases and platters with patterns that go back 1,000 years.

✛ E7 ✉ Calle de Isabel la Católica 2 ☎ 91 547 34 17 🚇 Santo Domingo

ANTIGUA PASTELERÍA DEL POZO

Spanish cakes may not be as delicate as French or Austrian pastries, but there are many with a tale to tell. This bakery dates back to 1830 and is known for its *roscones de Reyes*, a sweet bread associated with the Three Kings festival (6 January). But these rings of brioche-style bread, dotted with sugar and glazed fruits, are made on the premises year-round. Alternatively, go for the delicious tarts filled with pumpkin jam and custard. Closed Sun, mid-July to August.

✛ F7 ✉ Calle Pozo 8 ☎ 91 522 38 94 🚇 Sol

CASA DE DIEGO

This 150-year-old store is still the best place in Madrid to buy a real fan. They range from cheap and cheerful versions to exquisite hand-painted collector's items. The shop also sells umbrellas and walking sticks.

✛ F9 ✉ Plaza de la Puerta del Sol 12 ☎ 91 522 66 43 🚇 Sol

EL CORTE INGLÉS

www.elcorteingles.es
Spain's pride and joy, a department store that sells everything, and ensures good value for money.

WHAT'S ON OFFER?

The little specialist shops of Madrid can offer much insight into the minds of the city's inhabitants. Sometimes the shop's layout is so irrational that it is hard to know what the place is really selling. Particularly in the area around the Plaza Mayor, the district of La Latina and the area between Calle del Barco and Calle Hortaleza, just off the Gran Vía, it is worth pausing to admire off-beat window displays. These have been lovingly put together by proprietors who know they are as much a part of the urban landscape as any monument.

Some 20 stores in Madrid, including the flagship store on Calle de Preciados, just off the Puerta del Sol.

✛ F7 ✉ Calle de Preciados 1 ☎ 91 379 80 00 🚇 Sol

LA FAVORITA

The first top hats and bowler hats were sold here on the Plaza Mayor back in 1894. The shop survives and sells modern head gear, such as caps (*gorras*) and berets.

✛ F7 ✉ Plaza Mayor 25 ☎ 91 366 58 77 🚇 Sol

FELIX ANTIGÜEDADES

An antiques shop in the heart of the Rastro flea market where you'll find an intriguing collection of *objets d'art*, especially Oriental art and musical instruments.

✛ F9 ✉ Plaza General Vara del Rey 3 ☎ 91 365 60 98 🚇 La Latina

EL FLAMENCO VIVE

There is no doubt that flamenco lives inside Alberto Martínez's shop, Spain's first devoted to flamenco. In addition to a good selection of music, there are books on flamenco history and much flamenco paraphernalia.

✛ E7 ✉ Calle Conde de Lemos 7 ☎ 91 547 39 17 🚇 Opera

FNAC

Five floors of books and CDs, plus a small concert area. Also has foreign newspapers, photograph developing services and a ticket agency.

🗺 F7 ✉ Calle de Preciados 28 ☎ 90 210 06 32 🚇 Callao

GALERÍAS PIQUÉR

This pleasant mall in the Rastro street market has 20 antiques shops. Try Siglo 20 for art deco, and El Estudio for Isabelline furniture and lamps.

🗺 F9 ✉ Calle Ribera de Curtidores 29 🚇 La Latina, Rastro

GUANTES LUQUE

There's a vast range of gloves, with prices to suit every pocket, at 150-year-old store. Gloves come in wool, leather, cotton and silk, in myriad colors, for every occasion and every season of the year.

🗺 E8 ✉ Calle Espoz y Mina 3, Santa Ana ☎ 91 522 32 87 🚇 La Latina

GUITARRAS RAMÍREZ

www.guitarrasramirez.com

Since 1882, four generations of the Ramírez family have made and sold some of Spain's finest guitars which have been bought by amateurs as well as world-famous professional musicians from around the globe.

🗺 F7/8 ✉ Calle de la Paz 8 ☎ 91 531 42 29 🚇 Sol

MARIANO MADRUEÑO

www.marianomadrueno.es

The Spanish drink a wide range of their own wines, as well as unusual liqueurs such as *pacharán* (sloe gin). Barrels and alembics still decorate this century-old *bodega* (wine shop), near the Monasterio de las Descalzas Reales. It's still run by the same family and you will find the staff helpful with what is an eclectic selection.

🗺 F7 ✉ Calle Postigo de San Martín 3 ☎ 91 521 19 55 🚇 Callao

SESEÑA

www.sesena.com

With a firm eye on maintaining quality, this family establishment, dating back to 1901, specializes in capes. Pablo Picasso, Michael Jackson, and Hillary Clinton have all been customers.

🗺 F7/8 ✉ Calle de la Cruz 23 ☎ 91 531 68 40 🚇 Sol

SHOPPING AROUND

For better or worse, the retail scene in Madrid is increasingly dominated by chain stores and *centros comerciales* (shopping malls). Try to get into the back streets where you can visit smaller establishments. Shop assistants can be slow when it comes to serving customers they don't know, and 'service with a smile' is only now starting to catch on. Larger stores are open through lunch, while smaller ones continue to close from about 1.30 to about 4.30.

STAMPS AND COINS MARKET

People meet to discuss stamps and coins under the archways of the Plaza Mayor.

🗺 F7/8 ✉ Plaza Mayor 🕐 Sunday morning 🚇 Sol

LA VIOLETA

www.lavioletaonline.es

This tiny shop could be out of a fairy tale. It specializes in an unusual sweet: real sugared violets in jars and pretty little boxes. It also sells chocolates and candied fruits, and everything is wrapped beautifully.

🗺 F7 ✉ Plaza de Canalejas 6 ☎ 91 522 55 22 🚇 Sol

VIPS

www.clubvips.com

The 12 large, bright and bold VIPS stores dotted around the city sell books, magazines and CDs, along with food and gifts. Most are open 24 hours. Each also has a bar and restaurant.

🗺 F7 ✉ Gran Vía 65 (with branches throughout the city) ☎ 91 547 72 54 🚇 Callao

ZARA

www.zara.com

Now a household name around the world, Spanish chain Zara has five main-street stores in Madrid, offering stylish mainstream fashion for men and women at down-to-earth prices.

🗺 F7 ✉ Gran Vía 34 ☎ 91 521 12 83 🚇 Gran Vía

ARCO DE CUCHILLEROS

Top dancers and singers have performed for nearly 50 years at this *tablao flamenco*, close to the Plaza Mayor. It is more a bar with entertainment, so have a drink and watch the action between 9pm and 2am. Closed Monday.

E8 Calle Cuchilleros 7 91 364 02 63 Sol

BERLIN CABARET 1930

www.berlincabaret.com
The Spanish still love magic tricks, as well as the usual risqué song and dance, drag shows and high-kicking chorus lines. Expect lots of red velvet and a happy crowd. But, be warned: shows at this café-theater often start as late as 1am.

E8 Costanilla de San Pedro 11 91 366 20 34 Closed Mon La Latina, Ópera

LA BOCA DEL LOBO

'The Jaws of the Wolf' is a lively dance bar where the music can be anything from hip-hop to rock 'n' roll, depending on the DJ. Dark, smoky atmosphere. Open from 10pm till late.

G7/8 Calle Echegaray 11 91 468 17 91 Sevilla

CAFÉ CENTRAL

One of the best jazz venues in Europe. There are performances every night, mainly from Spanish, but sometimes foreign, musicians.

F8 Plaza del Ángel 10 91 369 41 43 Daily 10.30pm Sevilla, Antón Martín, Sol

CAFÉ POPULART

Live music every day— jazz, blues and swing—in a great environment with intelligent conversation.

G8 Calle Huertas 22 91 429 84 07 Antón Martín

LAS CARBONERAS

www.tablaslascarboneras.com
Madrid's newest flamenco club is already rated by aficionados for its quality acts. The show begins around 11pm, but arrive earlier if you want to be sure of a seat.

E8 Calle del Conde de Miranda 1 91 542 86 77 Sol

CASA PATAS

The best-known of Madrid's flamenco *tablaos* is a little touristy, but none the less enjoyable. Live midnight performances, more frequent in May.

F8 Calle Cañizares

RAVE ON

The limitless capacity of *madrileños* for having fun has made Madrid a dance club owner's dream. The city is the undisputed European nightlife capital, and the night begins and ends very late indeed.

10 91 369 15 74/04 96 Performances Thu–Sat midnight Tirso de Molina, Antón Martín

CERVECERÍA ALEMANA

www.cerveceriaalemana.com
One of the city's most popular bars. A good meeting place in the Santa Ana district.

F8 Plaza de Santa Ana 6 91 429 70 33 Antón Martín

CINE DORÉ

www.mcu.es/cine
A restored old cinema and now the seat of Filmoteca Española, the national film institute. Most of the films shown are in their original language with subtitles in Spanish. Even when there's nothing on, it has a good bar-restaurant and bookshop.

G8 Santa Isabel 3 91 369 11 25 Antón Martín

LE COCK

Round off the evening with a cocktail or two beneath the glass roof of this tastefully decorated late-night bar.

G7 Calle Reina 16 91 532 28 26 Banco de España

LA COQUETTE

The only Madrid bar dedicated exclusively to blues is very 1960s.

E/F7 Calle de las Hileras 14 91 530 80 95 Ópera

LA CORRALA

La Corrala is used for open-air *zarzuela* performances in summer.

F9 Calle Tribulete 12 No phone Lavapiés

GLASS BAR

A bar in the lobby of the Hotel Urban, with lots of glass, expensive cocktails and music that ranges from disco and soul to funky and pop.

G7 Carrera de San Jerónimo 34 Daily 11am–3am 91 787 77 70 Sol, Antón Martín

JOY ESLAVA (MADRID)

Plush, though not forbiddingly stylish, club in an 1850s theater. The central location attracts a diverse clientele.

F7 Calle Arenal 11 91 366 37 33 Ópera

PALACIO DE GAVIRIA

One of Madrid's more remarkable night-time locations. An 1851 palace, with fixtures and furniture generally intact, it reopened in 1981 as a nightspot. With its grand staircase entrance and 14 halls, it is well worth checking out.

F7 Calle Arenal 9 91 526 60 69 Sol

THE PENTHOUSE LOUNGE AND TERRACE

For spectacular views and equally spectacular cocktails, such as their very own Lavender Margarita,

head to the top floor of the hip new ME Madrid Reina Victoria Hotel.

F8 ME Madrid Hotel, Plaza de Santa Ana 14 Wed–Sat 9pm–4am, Sun 5pm–midnight 91 701 60 00 Sol, Antón Martín

EL SOL

www.elsolmad.com
Things start happening at El Sol around midnight and the pace gets faster through til 5am. Pay your €10 entry—which includes a drink—and dance till you drop to a mix of R'n'B, soul, funk and unmixed rock; great atmosphere, great people, but no frills.

F7 Calle Jardines 3 91 532 64 90 Gran Via, Sol

TEATRO MONUMENTAL

The place where classical concerts are recorded for broadcast by the Spanish Radio and Televison Orchestra and Choir.

ZARZUELA

In the words of Edmundo de Amici, writing in 1870, the *zarzuela* is 'a piece of music somewhere between comedy and melodrama, between opera and vaudeville, with prose and verse, both recited and sung, serious and lighthearted, a very Spanish and very entertaining musical form.' Among audiences of a certain age, it remains as popular as ever.

G8 Calle Atocha 65 91 429 12 81 Antón Martín

TEATRO DE LA ZARZUELA

www.teatrodelazarzuela.
mcu.es
Zarzuela, or light opera, is particularly popular with the older generation in Madrid. Even if you don't speak Spanish, the farcical plots are simple and easy to understand. The music and singing are top class. Enjoy it at this 150-year-old theater.

G7 Jovellanos 4 91 524 54 00 Varies, check schedule Antón Martín

TORRES BERMEJAS

www.torresbermejas.com
For over 40 years, this restaurant and club has hosted some of the most famous flamenco singers and dancers in the world. The setting is reminiscent of the Alhambra palace in Granada. Eat traditional Spanish dishes, such as *paella*, and then enjoy the show. More for tourists than locals.

F7 Mesonero Romanos 11 91 532 33 22 Callao

VIVA MADRID

The tiled *azulejo* frontage of Viva Madrid bar has been photographed for a thousand guide books.

G8 Calle Manuel Fernández y González 7 91 429 36 40 Antón Martín

PRICES

Prices are approximate, based on a 3-course meal for one person.

€€€	over €50
€€	€30–€50
€	under €30

BOTÍN (€€)

www.botin.es

Botín first opened its doors in 1725, making it, according to the *Guinness Book of Records*, the world's oldest restaurant. Suckling pig, roasted in a wood-fired oven, is the Castillian special dish.

🖪 E8 ⊠ Calle Cuchilleros 17 ☎ 91 366 42 17 🚇 La Latina

LOS CARACOLES (€)

How authentic do you want? This is all about snails: casseroled, with lots of garlic. Wash them down with a glass of draft vermouth. Eat standing up; feel like a local.

🖪 E9 ⊠ Calle de Toledo 106 ☎ 91 366 42 46 🕙 Tue–Sat 9am–11pm, Sun till 7.30pm 🚇 Puerta de Toledo

CASA ALBERTO (€€)

www.casaalberto.es

Characterful restaurant, founded in 1827, at the back of a bar that serves terrific tapas. It's full of bullfighting memorabilia. The ham croquettes and oxtail are recommended.

🖪 G8 ⊠ Calle Huertas 18 ☎ 91 429 93 56 🕙 Closed Sun night, Mon and 2 weeks in Aug 🚇 Antón Martín

CASA LABRA (€–€€)

www.casalabra.com

The Spanish Socialist Party was founded here in 1879, just 19 years after the bar was established, and Casa Labra has been producing typically *madrileño* tapas ever since. Tasty cod croquettes are a house specialty.

🖪 F7 ⊠ Calle Tetuán 12 ☎ 91 531 00 81 🚇 Sol

CERVECERÍA CERVANTES (€)

Packed with locals looking for the best fish and seafood tapas in town. Just point at what you fancy. The *tostada de gamba*, hot shrimps in aioli on toast, are quite delicious.

🖪 G8 ⊠ Plaza de Jesús 7 ☎ 91 429 60 93 🕙 Daily 11am–midnight. Closed Sun evening 🚇 Antón Martín

CHOCOLATERÍA SAN GINÉS (€)

Flashy, big and extremely busy, especially in winter.

NEW TASTES

For historical and geographical reasons, both Latin American and North African cuisines are increasingly popular on Madrid's hitherto fairly conservative culinary scene. The menus can be as incomprehensible to Spaniards as to any visitor. The best bet is to see what others are eating and order what looks appealing.

Three minutes from Sol.

🖪 F7 ⊠ Pasaje de San Ginés 5 ☎ 91 365 65 46 🚇 Sol, Ópera

ERROTA-ZAR (€€)

Opposite the Teatro de la Zarzuela, this has been one of the city's most authentic Basque restaurants for over 20 years. Specialties include fried fresh anchovies, tartare of bonito and a variety of traditional dishes using hake, string beans or mushrooms. As well as local cheeses, there are good desserts, such as chocolate cake and ice cream. The wine cellar has over 10,000 bottles.

🖪 G7 ⊠ Calle Jovellanos 3 (first floor) ☎ 91 531 25 64 🕙 Daily; closed Sun 🚇 Banco de España

LA ESQUINA DEL CAFÉ (€)

Tiny corner café that is known for its yummy desserts, such as *tiramisu* and chocolate cake. Ideal for a break from tapas, with a *café con leche* (coffee with hot milk).

🖪 G8 ⊠ Calle de Jesús 10 ☎ 91 369 30 84 🕙 Mon–Thu 12.30–5, Fri, Sat 12.30pm–2am, Sun 12.30–6 🚇 Antón Martín

LHARDY (€€–€€€)

www.lhardy.com

One of the city's classier restaurants and a local institution. The good range of fairly pricey tapas downstairs includes consommé, croquettes,

Russian salad on bread and, in summer, Madrid's best gazpacho. There is also a delicatessen.

⊞ F7 ✉ Calle Carrera de San Jerónimo 8 ☎ 91 521 33 85 ⏰ Closed Sun dinner, public hols 🚇 Sol

POSADA DE LA VILLA (€€€)

www.posadadelavilla.com
The building, just off the Plaza Mayor, dates back to 1642 and the atmosphere and dishes are about as traditional as you can get. This is the place to order Madrid oven-roast lamb and *cocido* (order 24 hours in advance).

⊞ E8 ✉ Cava Baja 9 ☎ 91 366 18 60 ⏰ Closed Sun dinner 🚇 Latina, Tirso de Molina, Sol

RESTAURANTE MOAÑA (€€€)

In an old-fashioned and rather formal setting, chef Francisco Romero Vieitez reworks traditional Galician recipes for fish and seafood. Choose from scallops, lobster, cod and more. Wide range of Galician wines.

⊞ E7 ✉ Calle de las Hileras 4 ☎ 91 548 29 14 ⏰ Closed Sun, dinner 🚇 Ópera

TABERNA DE ANTONIO SÁNCHEZ (€)

www.tabernaantoniosanchez.com
The best-conserved of all the tapas bars pays homage to the bullfighting family that has run it since 1830. Displays on bullfighting make the distinctive setting as fascinating as the tapas.

⊞ F8 ✉ Calle Mesón de Paredes 13 ☎ 91 539 78 26 🚇 Tirso de Molina

TABERNA MACEIRA (€)

Join the *madrileños* standing outside and wait for a table in this popular Galician-style haunt. Menus are on artists' palettes, the music is Galician bagpipes and the helpings are large: *pulpo* (octopus), *patatas bravas* (spicy potatoes) and jugs of sangría. Cramped, noisy, good value and good fun. Cash only, no reservations.

⊞ G8 ✉ Calle de las Huertas 66 ☎ 91 429 58 18 ⏰ Daily 1–4.30, 10.30–1 🚇 Antón Martín

MADRID GASTRONOMY

Madrid and its region have a distinctive style of cooking, which is plain, straightforward and tasty. *Asado* means roast, and there's nothing better than roast lamb or kid from a wood-fired oven. The other major local favorite is *cocido*, a stew with meat, chickpeas and vegetables. These are cooked together in a clay pot, right in the fireplace. Match these with the regional red wines made from Tempranillo grapes.

LA TAURINA (€)

www.lataurina.com
This is a shrine to bullfighting, with everything from bulls' heads and capes to sequined matador costumes and tiled murals of bullfights. But it is also a great place for tapas and heartier home-cooked Andalucian dishes, such as oxtail, gazpacho, black pudding, squid, tortilla and anchovies.

⊞ F7 ✉ Carrera de San Jerónimo 5 ☎ 91 531 39 69 ⏰ Daily 🚇 Sol

VINOTECA BARBECHERA (€)

www.vinoteca-barbechera.com
Part of a successful chain of wine bars, this is a good place to see modern Madrid at play. A good range of snacks is offered: platters of smoked tuna and trout, rolls stuffed with chorizo, ham or anchovies, crêpes for dessert, plus a wide range of wines by the glass from Spain and abroad. Six venues in Madrid, including one in Chueca.

⊞ G8 ✉ Calle del Príncipe 27 ☎ 91 420 04 78 ⏰ Daily 10am–midnight 🚇 Antón Martín, Sol

VIUDA DE VACAS (€)

Madrileños like to bring overseas visitors here for traditional Spanish cooking amid *azulejo* tiles and wooden tables.

⊞ E8 ✉ Calle Cava Alta 23 ☎ 91 366 58 47 ⏰ Closed Sun night 🚇 La Latina

With one of the world's most famous art museums and one of the world's great urban parks, this part of Madrid is a magnet for visitors. But don't miss the Real Fábrica de Tapices, the tapestry factory, where tradition rules.

Sights	70–77
Shopping	78
Entertainment and Nightlife	79
Restaurants	79–80

Jerónimos and the East

SALAMANCA

Hermosilla

Velázquez

GOYA

La Concepción

Archivo
Heráldico

CALLE

PRÍNCIPE

DE

VERGARA

Calle del General Pardiñas

Príncipe de
Vergara

Calle de Castelló

ALCALÁ

DE

O'DONNELL

Puerta de
Madrid

Plaza
Costa Rica

Glorieta
Sevilla

Bolivia

Colombia

Plaza de
Guatemala

Glorieta
Sardana

AVENIDA

DE

Paseo del Duque de Fernán Núñez

Calle Antonio Acuña

Paseo de Venezuela

Jardines del
Arquit Herrero
Palacios

Palacio de
Velázquez

Palacio
de Cristal

MENÉNDEZ

Y

PELAYO

Jardines
de Cecilio
Rodríguez

Hospital del
Niño Jesús

*Parque
del Retiro*

Paseo de Uruguay

Glorieta
del Ángel
Caído

La
Rosaleda

Paseo del Duque de Fernán Núñez

Puerta
Granada

Puerta del
Pacífico

Calle Poeta Esteban Villegas

DE

MENÉNDEZ

Y

PELAYO

Calle de Reyes Magos

Calle Andrés

Plaza
Mariano
de Cavia

CRISTINA

PACÍFICO

Torrejón

Calle de
Gutenberg

AVENIDA

Real Fábrica
de Tapices

J

K

L

Museo del Prado

HIGHLIGHTS

● *Las Meninas,* Velázquez
● Goya's 'dark paintings'
● *The 2nd of May, The 3rd of May, Las Majas,* Goya
● *The Holy Family,* Raphael
● *The Bacchanal, Emperor Charles V in Mühlberg,* Titian
● *The Garden of Earthly Delights,* Bosch
● *The Triumph of Death,* Brueghel
● *Self Portrait,* Dürer
● *David and Goliath,* Caravaggio
● *The Three Graces,* Rubens

TIPS

● Weekends are always crowded; plan to go first thing in the morning, or at the end of the day.
● The Casón del Buen Retiro houses the Prado's collection of 19th-century art.

The city's pride in the magnificent Prado is justified. With its Goyas, El Grecos and other masterpieces, it is undoubtedly one of the great art museums of the world.

Brief history The neoclassical building, completed by Juan de Villanueva in 1785, was conceived by Charles III as a center for the study of natural sciences. After Napoléon's troops damaged it during the Spanish Wars of Succession, it was restored by Fernando VII as a home for the royal collection of paintings and sculptures and opened as a museum in November 1819. It is unequaled in the world, with a collection numbering 7,000 pictures, of which around 1,500 are on display at any given time; there are 115 Goyas, 83 works by Rubens, 50 by Velázquez, 40 Brueghels, 36 Titians, 32 El

The Museo del Prado has over 1,500 paintings on diplay, but don't miss those by Goya, Velázquez, El Greco, Brueghel and Titian

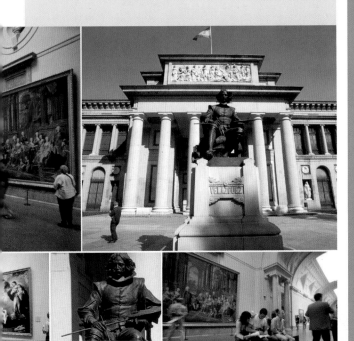

Grecos and 20 Zurbaráns. With the opening of the extension in 2007 and that of the Cason del Buen Retiro in 2012, the museum gained much-needed space for temporary exhibitions. The Prado is best appreciated in more than one visit.

Velázquez and Goya Do not leave the Prado without seeing Velázquez's masterpiece, Las Meninas, widely considered technically the finest painting in the world. Goya's Majas—two paintings believed to be of the Duchess of Alba, one naked, one clothed—positively beckon the spectator into the picture, Madrid's seductive answer to the Mona Lisa. Goya's pinturas negras—among them Saturn Devouring One of his Sons and Half-Drowned Dog—are obviously the work of a man whose sanity is in decline. At once grotesque, disturbing and breathtaking, they are unique.

THE BASICS

www.museoprado.es
H8
Paseo del Prado
Mon–Sat 10–8, Sun and public hols 10–7
91 330 28 00
Restaurant, café
Atocha, Recoletos
Banco de España, Atocha 9, 10, 14, 19, 27, 34, 37, 45
Expensive. Free to under 18s, students 18–25. Also free Mon–Sat 6–8pm, Sun and public hols 5–7pm (temporary exhibitions only)

Parque del Retiro

Small enough to be welcoming, but large enough to get pleasantly lost in, the Retiro will linger in your memory, particularly if you see it in late spring or early autumn, when its colors are most vivid.

History On a sunny Sunday afternoon, the whole city seems drawn to the Retiro park, 1.2sq km (0.5sq miles) in the city center, whose name translates as 'retreat'. Originally thickly wooded and once a hunting ground for Philip II, the Retiro was the brainchild of the Duke of Olivares, who designed it in the 1630s for Philip IV as part of the Buen Retiro Palace—a complex of royal buildings and immense formal gardens that inspired Louis XIV at Versailles. It was used until the time of Charles III, who partially opened it to the public in the 1770s. Most of the palace was destroyed during the Napoleonic Wars.

A walk in the park Use the entrance on Calle Alfonso XII, opposite the Casón del Buen Retiro. Walk through the parterre gardens and up the steps along a broad, shady avenue to the lake. If you want to take a boat out, head left around the lake; opposite you is a statue of Alfonso XII, a popular spot to soak up the sun. Otherwise, turn right and follow the Paseo de Republica de Cuba. From here, you can take one of many paths leading to the Palacio de Cristal (Glass Palace), the Retiro's loveliest building. Constructed in 1886, it is one of several exhibition spaces within the park. At the southern end of the park is La Rosaleda (the Rose Garden), in full glory in May.

THE BASICS

⊞ H7–J8

✉ Calle Alcalá, Alfonso XII, Avenida de Menedez Pelayo, Paseo de la Reina Cristina

🕐 May–Sep 6am–midnight; Oct–Apr 6am–10pm

🍴 Terrazas

🚇 Atocha, Retiro

🚉 Retiro, Atocha, Ibiza

🚌 2, 19, 20, 26, 28, 52, 148

HIGHLIGHTS

● Palacio de Cristal
● Artichoke Fountain in the Rose Garden
● Cecilio Rodríguez Gardens
● Velázquez Palace
● Statue of Alfonso XII
● Lake
● Fallen Angel statue
● 400-year-old cypress tree near Philip IV entrance
● Philip IV parterre
● Observatory (1790)
● Free band concerts from May to October
● Puppet shows for children on Sunday

Plaza de la Cibeles

The fountain of La Cibeles, on Plaza de la Cibeles (left and right)

THE BASICS

➕ H7
✉ Plaza de la Cibeles
🚇 Atocha, Recoletos
🚌 Banco de España
🚍 5, 9, 10, 14, 20, 27, 34, 45, 51, 53 and all night buses

HIGHLIGHTS

● Post Office
● Gardens of Palacio de Linares
● Facade of Bank of Spain building
● Robert Michel's lions
● Newspaper stand on Paseo del Prado

Despite the constant traffic, this plaza, a sheer mass of stone around a dramatic statue of the fertility goddess, La Cibeles, is Madrid's most overwhelming square.

Cars pass by Seated imperiously at one of Madrid's busiest intersections, the goddess and her marble fountain were erected according to instructions from Charles III (1716–88). The main statue is by Francisco Gutiérrez and the lions, Hipponomes and Atlanta, drawing the goddess' chariot, are by Robert Michel. Originally at the corner of the square, the statue was finally completed in 1792 and moved in 1895, at which date the cherubim were added.

Around the plaza The enormous wedding-cake look-alike on the southeastern side of the square is one of Madrid's most imposing buildings. It was designed by Antonio Palacios in 1904, its painstakingly worked facade reminiscent of Viennese style. Designed by Antonio Palacios in 1904 to be the Palacio de Comunicaciones (Central Post Office), it was dubbed by local wits as Our Lady of Communications, as if it were a cathedral. The building is now used by the Madrid City Council.

The Palacio de Linares The real treasure of the Plaza de la Cibeles is the elaborately decorated Palacio de Linares. It was designed in 1872, and restored and opened in 1992 as the Casa de América. It now showcases exhibits about Latin American visual arts.

If you are traveling from the airport by taxi to Madrid's center, this gateway is one of the first things you will see. It is perhaps the city's most powerful emblem, particularly when lit at night.

Neoclassical symbol Listed as a National Monument, the Puerta de Alcalá, in the Plaza de la Independencia, is one of the great symbols of Madrid. It is perhaps the city's finest example of the neoclassical architecture that came as a reaction to previous baroque excesses. Commissioned by Charles III, who was to be responsible for much of the city's architectural transformation, it was designed by Francisco Sabatini in 1778 as the main entrance to the Court. Best appreciated when floodlit at night, the Puerta de Alcalá stands in the middle of a traffic junction, and is best admired from a distance.

Design Five arches of granite and stone, the statue has 10 columns similar to those used by Michelangelo for the Capitol in Rome—facing east and crowned with Ionic capitals. Three central archways are flanked by two smaller ones. The lion heads in the middle of the three higher arches are the work of Robert Michel, and the cherubim, the trophies and the coat of arms that surmount the statue are by Francisco Gutiérrez. You can still see the bullet marks from the 1921 assassination attempt on Eduardo Dato, President of Madrid's Council of Ministers, on the north side of the statue. Luckily, a Madrid Town Council proposal to paint parts of the *puerta* white was rejected.

THE BASICS

➕ H7
✉ Plaza de la Independencia
🚇 Recoletos
🚊 Retiro
🚌 9, 15, 20, 28, 51, 52

HIGHLIGHTS

● Views of the monument when lit at night
● The lion heads designed by Robert Michel
● Bullet holes from a 1921 assassination attempt

More to See

CASÓN DEL BUEN RETIRO

www.museoprado.es

This was originally the ballroom of the Buen Retiro Royal Palace, a building destroyed by Napoleonic troops but rebuilt by Charles III, who had the vault decorated with frescoes. It holds free temporary exhibitions.

➕ H8 ✉ Calle Alfonso XII 68 ☎ 902 10 70 77 🚇 Retiro, Banco de España 🚌 9, 10, 14, 27, 37, 45

ESTACIÓN DE ATOCHA

A vast indoor tropical garden can be found inside this late 19th-century wrought-iron station canopy by Alberto del Palacio. The cylindrical glass tower nearby is a monument to the 191 victims of the 11 March, 2004 bomb attacks on Madrid trains.

➕ H9 ✉ Plaza del Emperador Carlos V ☎ 90 210 00 07 🚇 Atocha 🚌 14, 27, 34, 37, 45 ♿ Few

JARDINES DEL DESCUBRIMIENTO

Typical of Madrid circa1970s, these sculpture gardens in the Plaza de Colón were built to celebrate Spain's role in the discovery of the New World. There is an 1892 Jerónimo Suñol statue of Christopher Columbus, but the real highlight here are the Joaquín Vaquero Turcios sculptures. Beneath the gardens is the Centro Cultural de la Villa de Madrid.

➕ H6 ✉ Plaza de Colón 🚇 Recoletos 🚌 1, 5, 9, 14, 19, 21, 27, 37, 45, 51, 53, 74, 89

MUSEO ARQUEOLÓGICO NACIONAL

Spain's national archaeological museum is closed for refurbishment but a 'best of' selection from the collection, including many fabulous finds from Prehistoric times and the Middle Ages, is open in the meantime.

➕ H6 ✉ Calle de Serrano 🚇 Serrano, Retiro 🚌 1, 9, 19, 51, 74

PLAZA DE LA LEALTAD

A stone's throw from the Prado, this elegant, semicircular plaza dominated by the Ritz Hotel has an obelisk in the middle to the memory of those

Estación de Atocha

Casón del Buen Retiro

who died at the hands of Napoleonic troops on 3 May 1808. Their ashes are kept in an urn at the base of the monument. The Madrid Stock Exchange was built here in 1884, in a neoclassical design that neatly echoes the Prado.

🔳 H7 ✉ Plaza de la Lealtad 🚇 Banco de España 🚌 10, 14, 27, 34, 37, 45

REAL FÁBRICA DE TAPICES

www.realfabricadetapices.com
The centuries-old craft of creating tapestries and carpets continues in the Royal Tapestry Factory. The looms still hum as they did in the 18th century, when the Flemish van der Goten family founded the works. On the tour (40 minutes) you learn that many of the original designs were created by Goya and other famous artists, and that it can take four months to finish one square meter.

🔳 J9 ✉ Calle de Fuenterrabía 2 ☎ 91 434 05 50 🕐 Mon–Fri 10–2. Closed Sat, Sun, Holy Week, Aug 🚇 Atocha, Menéndez Pelayo 🚌 14, 24, 26, 32, 37, 54, 141 ⚿ None 💵 Inexpensive

REAL JARDÍN BOTÁNICO

www.rjb.csic.es
These peaceful gardens are the result of overseas expeditions in search of interesting species dating back to the 18th century. The plants and trees are carefully classified and laid out along geometrical walkways. It's the perfect retreat from the city.

🔳 H8 ✉ Plaza de Murillo 2 🕐 Daily from 10am; closing varies with season 🚇 Atocha 🚌 10, 14, 27, 34, 37, 45 💵 Inexpensive

SAN JERÓNIMO EL REAL

Iglesia de San Jerónimo el Real, Madrid's society church, wedged at the side of the Prado, was built back in 1505, but over the centuries renovations included several controversial neo-Gothic additions. The steps at the entrance on Calle Alarcón, for example, were built especially for the wedding of Alfonso XIII and his queen, Victoria Eugenia, in 1906.

🔳 H8 ✉ Calle Moreto 4 ☎ 91 420 35 78 🕐 Daily 10–1, 5–8 🚇 Atocha, Banco de España ⚿ Difficult 💵 Free

Craftspeople at work in the Royal Tapestry Factory

Shopping

CORONEL TAPIOCCA
www.coroneltapiocca.com
A chain aimed at the modern-day adventurer, selling everything from rucksacks, trousers and fishing gear to camping and hunting equipment. Although designed for comfort, the clothes are sporty and stylish.
H9 ✉ Estacion Atocha s/n ☎ 91 826 60 23 🚇 Atocha

FABENDI
Established for over 30 years, this is a shop that locals head for when they want something—anything—in leather: leather and suede coats, jackets, trousers and even suits.
K9 ✉ Avenida del Mediterráneo 5 ☎ 91 552 24 14 🚇 Menéndez Pelayo

GALERÍA DE ARTE VICTORIA HIDALGO
www.victoriahidalgo.com
A step away from the Prado museum. Ever since 1998, this gallery has shown paintings and sculptures by living artists.
H8 ✉ Calle de Ruiz de Alarcón 27 ☎ 91 429 56 65 🚇 Banco de España

IMAGINARIUM
www.imaginarium.es
Much more than a children's toy shop, this is all about what the name promises: imagination. From musical toys to dolls, the idea is to encourage children to have fun, in a creative,
yet educational way. Think inflatable city—with skyscrapers.
H9 ✉ Plaza del Emperador Carlos V ☎ 91 506 21 23 🚇 Atocha

EL JARDÍN DE SERRANO
www.jardindeserrano.es
Select shopping mall in two restored 19th-century mansions on the corner of *calles* Goya and Serrano. The well-heeled stores inside sell fashion, jewelry, gifts, toys and accessories.
H6 ✉ Calle de Goya 6–8 ☎ 91 577 00 12 🚇 Serrano

MUSEO DEL PRADO
www.tiendaprado.com
The museum's excellent Palacios y Museos shop is a great place to find quality souvenirs. As well as fine reproductions of famous works, there are silk scarves and blouses, pictures and chocolates, ties and jewelry.
H8 ✉ Paseo del Prado

WHERE TO GO
Madrid's amazing array of antique shops are in three main areas: the *barrio* Salamanca, around the Calle del Prado and Santa Ana, and around the Rastro, particularly down the Calle Ribera de Curtidores—the most likely source for bargains. Many shops do not specialize in any particular goods, but sell a broad selection of merchandise.

☎ 91 330 28 00 🚇 Banco de España

NATURA SELECTION
www.naturaselection.es
Dedicated to arts and crafts, plus clothes from South America, Asia and Africa. All are one of a kind, with scarves and bags, lamps and gloves—all made of natural materials such as cotton, silk and leather.
H9 ✉ Plaza del Emperador Carlos V ☎ 91 467 21 28 🚇 Atocha

PERFUMERÍA ALVAREZ GOMEZ
www.alvarezgomez.com
There are branches of this long-established perfumery all over Madrid. They sell a huge range of cosmetics and scents, but mostly their own delicate, flowery fragrances and colognes, beautifully bottled and excellent value.
H6 ✉ Calle de Serrano 14 ☎ 91 431 16 56 🚇 Retiro

PIEL DE TORO
www.pieldetoro.com
This is a trendy Madrid souvenir shop for adults as well as children where you can buy the famous must-have T-shirts, with a design that looks like a bull, and also like the outline of Spain. Almost directly opposite the Jardín Botánico.
H8 ✉ Paseo del Prado 42 ☎ 91 360 07 52 🚇 Atocha

Entertainment and Nightlife

DISCOTECA AZÚCAR
www.azucarsalsadisco.com
Even if you cannot dance the salsa, you can have lessons every night at this popular Latin American club where the music is persistent and the crowd is full of fun.
🔳 J9 ✉ Calle Atocha 107 ☎ 91 402 16 40 ⏰ Daily 11pm–5.30am, Fri, Sat 11.30pm–6.30am 🚇 Atocha

FLORIDA PARK
www.floridaparkdisco.com
Just inside the gates on the eastern side of the Retiro Park, Florida Park has long been a popular destination for out-of-town visitors. With a restaurant, dance floor and stage, this suits those who enjoy a show and dancing late into the night.
🔳 J7 ✉ Avenida de

Menéndez Pelayo (at Ibiza) ☎ 91 573 78 04 ⏰ Daily 9pm–3am. Closed Sun, Mon 🚇 Ibiza

KAPITAL
www.grupo-kapital.com
With its seven floors of dancing, this could be the

> ### MADRID BY NIGHT
>
> With almost 4,000 places to have a drink, Madrid can claim to be Europe's finest city for sheer variety of late-night options—sometimes very late indeed. Main bar areas in the center are the start of the Paseo de la Castellana (sophisticated), Malasaña (thoroughly unsophisticated), La Latina and Santa Ana (somewhere in between), and Chueca (gay).

biggest club in Madrid. There is everything from salsa, house and karaoke to R'n'B, go-go dancers and a cinema. The great attraction in summer is the rooftop terrace. Although teenagers dominate in the early evening, grown-ups flood in later, when the dress code is smart-casual.
🔳 H9 ✉ Calle de Atocha 125 ☎ 91 420 29 06 ⏰ Fri, Sat 5.30pm–10.30pm, Thu–Sun midnight–6am 🚇 Atocha

EL RETIRO
Sundays in the park (▷ 73) are famous for the entertainers and musicians who keep old and young amused. Outstanding are the summer concerts, called *Veranos de la Villa*.

Restaurants

> ### PRICES
>
> Prices are approximate, based on a 3-course meal for one person.
> €€€ over €50
> €€   €30–€50
> €   under €30

EL BOTÁNICO (€€€)
www.restaurantebotanico.com
A block from the Prado, this peaceful bar-restaurant has a shady *terraza* and elegantly traditional

and spacious interior. The menu offers solid Spanish specialties, as well as pasta dishes, salads and tapas. Excellent fish and home-style desserts.
🔳 H7 ✉ Calle ruiz de Alarcón 27 ☎ 91 420 23 42 ⏰ Mon–Fri 8–midnight, Sat and Sun 8–1am 🚇 Banco de España

LA CASTELA (€€)
www.lacastela.com
A local favorite, this typical *taberna* is part

tapas bar and part dining room specializing in Spanish cuisine.
🔳 K7 ✉ Calle del Doctor Castelo 22 ☎ 91 573 55 90 ⏰ Daily 2–4, 9–midnight. Closed Sun, Aug 🚇 Ibiza, Príncipe de Vergara

LA GAMELLA (€€€)
www.lagamella.com
On the first floor of a splendid old building that was the birthplace of Spanish philosopher José Ortega y Gasset, this

small American-owned restaurant is across from the Retiro. Here 'fusion' cooking mixes Spanish and American at the top end of the range: steak tartare with a shot of Jack Daniels, a classic Caesar salad and proper burgers.

🚩 H7 ✉ Calle de Alfonso XII 4 ☎ 91 532 45 09 🕔 Daily 1.30pm–4, 9–late. Closed Sat lunch, Sun 🚇 Retiro

LA HOJA (€€)

www.lahoja.es

Free-range chicken is the base of much of the cooking at this straightforward, but elegant family-run restaurant, where the emphasis is on Asturian-style recipes. Not one for vegetarians.

🚩 K7 ✉ Calle del Doctor Castelo 48 ☎ 91 409 25 22 🕔 Daily 1pm–midnight. Closed Sun, Mon dinner 🚇 Ibiza, Príncipe de Vergara

INDICE RESTAURANT AT AC PALACIO DEL RETIRO (€€€)

www.ac-hotels.com

Chef David Herranz takes hotel dining to a new level in this smart, contemporary setting. This chef is known for his delicate touch, and for giving a modern twist to traditional Mediterranean dishes. Topped off with an outstanding wine list.

🚩 H7 ✉ Ac Palacio del Retiro Hotel, Calle de Alfonso XII 14 ☎ 91 523 74 60 🕔 Daily lunch, dinner 🚇 Retiro, Banco de España

RESTAURANTE VIRIDIANA (€€€)

www.restauranteviridiana.com

At one of Madrid's finest restaurants, Abraham García is known as a character, but he is also a very fine cook, preparing complex modern dishes using traditional and high-quality Spanish produce. The wine list is one of the best in the city.

🚩 H7 ✉ Calle de Juan de Mena 14 ☎ 91 531 10 39 🕔 Daily 1.30–4, 8.30–midnight 🚇 Banco de España, Retiro

RITZ HOTEL (€€)

www.ritzmadrid.com

What could be more traditional than tea at the Ritz? In the Lobby Bar, listen to the pianist, harp-

TAPAS

The tapa, a snack to accompany your drink, is a part of Spanish culture. It started in the 18th century when Carlos III insisted that his entourage cover their wine with a plate of food to keep dust from getting into it (*tapa* means 'lid'). Many bars no longer display their wares, which can make it hard to order; it's easier when the tapas are kept behind glass so you can see them before buying. Pay before leaving, rather than on a round-by-round basis. Many *cervecerías* (late-night bars) sell tapas and make an atmospheric venue for a night-time snack.

ist or classical Spanish guitarist as you sip tea and nibble elegant sandwiches and scones. In summer, the experience is even nicer—take a wicker chair in the garden for lunch, tapas or dinner.

🚩 H7 ✉ Plaza de la Lealtad 5 ☎ 91 701 67 67 🕔 Daily 4.30–7pm 🚇 Banco de España

SULA ÁLBORA (€€–€€€)

Star chef Quique Dacosta's ultra-cool geometric bar, restaurant and luxury gourmet food shop is geared to leading-edge fashion food. Every dish—from salads, carpaccios and the finest Spanish hams to pastas and desserts—is a treat for the eye. The wine cellar is one of the city's best.

🚩 J6 ✉ Calle de Jorge Juan 33 ☎ 91 781 61 97 🕔 Daily noon–midnight 🚇 Velázquez, Retiro

TRATTORIA SANT'ARCANGELO (€€)

www.trattoriasantarcangelo.es

In a semi-basement, just a few steps from the Prado and the Jardín Botánico, this is rated as one of Madrid's best and most authentic, Italian restaurants. Carefully prepared dishes include crispy pizzas, spaghetti with a rich seafood sauce and tiramisu.

🚩 H8 ✉ Calle de Moreto 15 ☎ 91 369 10 93 🕔 Daily 🚇 Banco de España

Although it is known as the city's gay area, Chueca is open to all, with a variety of fun restaurants. Then there is Malasaña; considered clubland by many youngsters, this area is being gentrified.

Chueca and the North

This is a map. The following labels and place names are visible:

Grid references (edges): 2, 3, 4, 5, 6, 7 (left side); F, G, H (bottom)

Calle Carbonero y Sol
C. de Grijalba
Calle Maestro Ripoll
PASEO DE LA CASTELLANA
CALLE DE VITRUVIO
Calle de Agustín de Betancourt
Ministerio Trabajo y S Social
Ministerio de Medio Ambiente
Calle de Cristóbal Bordiú
Museo de Geología
CALLE DE RÍOS ROSAS
RÍOS ROSAS
Botero Statues
Plaza de San Juan de la Cruz
Museo Nacional de Ciencias Naturales
CALLE DE SANTA ENGRACIA
CALLE MURILLO
Sala del Canal de Isabel II
Parque Santa Engracia
Ríos Rosas
CHAMBERÍ
Ponzano
Cano
Calle de Lafuente
Espronceda
Ministerio Defensa
Calle de la Hoz
de los
Herreros
Zurbano
Monumento de Isabel La Católica
Calle
Canal
CALLE DE BRAVO
CALLE
JOSÉ
ABASCAL
Plaza Dr Marañón
CALLE
Calle de García de Paredes
Calle Santísima Trinidad
Calle General Álvarez de Castro
Alonso Cano
Convento San Vicente
Calle Fernández
García de Paredes
Gregorio Marañón
CALLE DE MIGUEL
Viriato
Museo Sorolla
Glorieta Emilio Castelar
Calle Feijoo
Sinagoga
Glorieta Pintor Sorolla
PASEO GENERAL MARTÍNEZ CAMPOS
ALMAGRO
TRAFALGAR
CALLE ELOY GONZALO
Iglesia
Calle Sagunto
Convento Esclavas del Sagrado Corazón
de
Rafael
ÁNGEL
Calvo
Fortuny
Museo Escultura Aire Lib
Glorieta de Quevedo
Magallanes
Calle de García Álvarez de Castro
Calle del Cardenal
Calle Jordán
Plaza de Olavide
Calle Santa Feliciana
Calle de Raimundo Lulio
PASEO DE EDUARDO DATO
Glorieta Rubén Darío
Pte Enrique de la Mata Gorostizaga
Calle Olid
Trafalgar
Garcilaso
Calle del General Arrando
Rubén Darío
Calle Jenner
CALLE DE SAN BERNARDO
Monteleón
Calle de Palafox
Calle Manuel Silvela
San José de la Montaña
Calle de Caracas
Calle Marqués Riscal
CALLE DE LA CASTELLANA
Ruiz
Cisneros
LUCHANA
CALLE DE SANTA ENGRACIA
Monasterio Convento Visitación Santa María
Calle de Zurbarán
Paseo de la Castellana
Calle de Sandoval
Bilbao
Nicasio Gallego
CALLE CARRANZA
Glorieta Bilbao
Malasaña
CALLE DE SAGASTA
Plaza Alonso Martínez
Calle Fernando El Santo
Monte
Calle de Churruca
Calle de Larra
Calle Serrano Anguita
Calle Mejía Lequerica
Alonso Martínez
Calle de Manuela
Calle de Andrés
FUENCARRAL
Calle del divino Pastor
Plaza de Dos de Mayo
Museo de Arquie Riv Historia
Jardines
CALLE DE SAN MATEO
Museo del Romanticismo
JUSTICIA
CALLE DE GÉNOVA
Colón
Plaza de Colón
Calle de la Palma
Tribunal
Vicente Ferrer
San
HORTALEZA
Calle de Argensola
Calle General Castaños
Palacio de Justicia
Santa Bárbara
Museo de Cera
Calle del Tesoro
Espíritu
Marqués de Santa Ana
Calle Jesús del Valle
Santo
Calle de la Madera
Calle San Lorenzo
Calle Santa Brígida
Iglesia de San Antón
Calle Fernando VI
Calle Belén
Calle Barbará de Braganza
Calle Marqués de la Ensenada
Convento de San Plácido
San Antonio Alemanes
Calle del Valverde
Calle corredera
Calle de San Pablo
Calle de Piamonte
Calle del Almirante
Calle de Prim
Chueca
Calle de Augusto Figueroa
Gravina
Barquillo
PASEO DE RECOLETOS
Casa de las Siete Chimeneas
Calle de San Bartolomé
San
Marcos
Plaza del Rey
de las Infantas
Palacio de Buenavista
Banco de España

Scale: 0 — 250 m / 0 — 250 yds

Plaza de la República Argentina

EL VISO

República Argentina

CALLE DE RODRÍGUEZ MARÍN

Calle Zurbarán

Calle Gallizza

Calle de Zabaleta

Auditorio Nacional de Música

Calle

Calle de Cartagena

Espíritu Santo

Calle DE VELÁZQUEZ

CALLE DE JOAQUÍN COSTA

Calle de Felipe Lobo

Calle J.R. Jiménez

Calle Gabriel Lobo

Villa de Campos

Calle de la Torre

VERGARA

DE

PRÍNCIPE

Cruz del Rayo

CALLE DE CARTAGENA

General Cabrera

Zabala

Calle Pablo Aranda

CALLE

DE

Calle Antonio

Calle Pérez

Calle San Julio

Miguel de los Santos

Calle de G. Luis

Calle de Cartagena

Calle de Quintiliano

Cantillos

Archivo Histórico Nacional

Calle Castillón de la prada

HOYOS

Glorieta López de Hoyos

CALLE

Calle Pinilla del Valle

Calle San Fernando de Jarama

de

Pedro

DE

Valdivia

AVENIDA DE AMÉRICA

MARÍA

LÓPEZ

DE

MOLINA

Avenida de América

DE FRANCISCO

Gimnasio Moscardó

Calle de Coslada

DE

Museo Lázaro Galdiano

VELÁZQUEZ

Castelló

VERGARA

Calle

Coello

Lagasca

del

General

Santa Mónica

Oráa

Pardiñas

SILVELA

Convento P Dominicos

CALLE

Balboa

DIEGO

DE

Diego de León

LEÓN

General Díaz

Porlier

SERRANO

San Francisco de Borja

Calle

de

Núñez

DE

La Virgen Peregrino

Calle de Maldonado

General

CASTELLANA

Museo de Arte Infantil

Núñez de Balboa

CALLE

DE

JUAN

BRAVO

Maldonado

CALLE DE JUAN BRAVO

Calle

Calle

de

Padilla

PRÍNCIPE

DE

Ntra Sra del Pilar

San Andrés Flamencos

Calle

Padilla

Calle de Padilla

Calle

DE

JOSÉ

ORTEGA

Y

GASSET

Fundación Juan March

Castelló

Plaza Marqués de Salamanca

CALLE DE JOSÉ ORTEGA Y GASSET

Coello

Lagasca

Don

Ramón

Balboa

de

la

Núñez de Balboa

Rosario

Calle

de

Claudio

Calle

de

Santa M de Monte Carmelo

Ramón

de

Núñez

Cruz

VERGARA

Ayala

Calle

de

Ayala

PRÍNCIPE DE

Chueca and the North

J

K

Museo Lázaro Galdiano

HIGHLIGHTS

● *Landscape*, Gainsborough
● *St. John in Patmos*, Bosch
● *Luis de Góngora*, Velázquez
● *The Adoration of the Magi*, El Greco

TIP

● Take one of the free guided tours on Sat or Sun at 11.30am.

There cannot be many museums like this wonderful oddity, which is surprisingly unfamiliar to many *madrileños*. Every time you go there is something new to discover in this dazzling collection.

A noble art collector José Lázaro Galdiano was born into Navarre nobility and became an obsessive, seemingly unfocused art collector, who died in 1947 at the age of 85. He married Paola Florido, an Argentinian who shared his love for art, and together they devoted their lives to traveling the world in search of treasures. An essentially private man, Galdiano never revealed how much he paid for any of the masterpieces. On his death, he donated his collection to the state, and the museum opened in 1951. Now completely reorganized, the exhibition begins on

Portrait of a Lady *by Thomas Gainsborough* (left); The Crusaders before Jerusalem *by Velázquez (right)*

the ground floor with an assessment of Lázaro's role as patron and collector and displays a representative sample of the collection, which includes paintings by Hieronymus Bosch, Bartolomé Murillo, Rembrandt, Francisco Zurbarán, El Greco, Velázquez, José de Ribera, Turner and Goya, as well as exquisite gold and silverwork, enamelwork, bronzes, medieval stained glass, jewelry, fans and weaponry.

Parque Florido The collection is housed in the Parque Florido, a neo-Renaissance palazzo named after Lázaro's wife. The beautifully restored interiors provide a magnificent setting for the treasures on display. Don't miss the spectacular painted ceilings, commissioned by Lázaro to decorate what were originally the family's private apartments. This is the finest of Madrid's smaller art galleries.

THE BASICS

www.flg.es

🕂 J4

✉ Serrano 122

☎ 91 561 60 84

🕓 Mon, Wed–Sat 10–4.30, Sun 10–3

🚇 Nuñez de Balboa/ Rubén Dario, Gregorio Marañón

🚌 9, 12, 16, 19, 51

♿ Good

💰 Moderate. Reduced price for over 60s and students. Free Wed–Sat, and Mon 3.30–4.30, Sun 2–3

Museo Sorolla

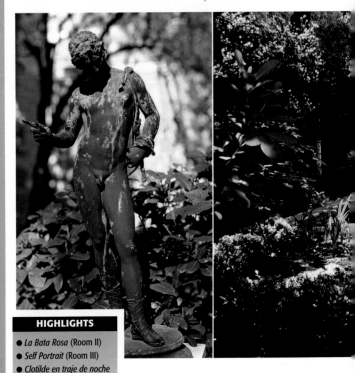

This serene spot belonged to Spain's finest Impressionist, Valencian Joaquín Sorolla, who wanted to create an oasis of peace for himself in a busy city. It is the best of Madrid's house museums.

Entrance and gardens The Sorolla Museum is one of the few places in the city to give us a sense of the shape of an artist's life and work. Built in 1910–11 by Enrique María de Repollés, it was the Madrid home of Joaquín Sorolla (1863–1923) and became a museum after Sorolla's widow, Clotilde, donated it to the state. It was opened to the public in 1932. The two small gardens, designed by Sorolla himself as a setting for his collection of fountains and fonts, are a bit of Andalucía in Madrid. The first is an imitation of a part of the Seville *alcázar*, while the second is

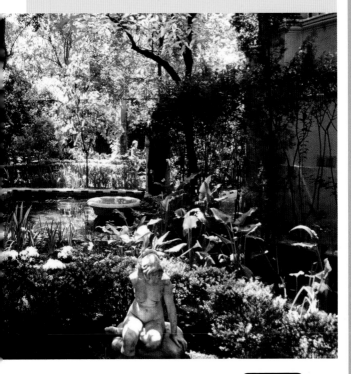

modeled on the Generalife Gardens in Granada's Alhambra. Near the entrance is a replica of a white marble bust of Sorolla by Mariano Benlliure, and to the left is an Andalucian patio.

Inside Lovingly preserved, the house is filled with turn-of-the-20th-century elegance. The ground floor, with its salon and dining room, gives a real feeling of the artist's life and displays his collection of antique pottery. The upper floor has been converted into a gallery, each room given over to a different aspect of Sorolla's work. Be sure to visit his studio, complete with a Turkish bed for the afternoon siesta. Among the paintings here are several of his wife, Clotilde. Although some see a fairy-tale, picture-postcard quality in his art, there is no denying the brilliance of his handling of light.

THE BASICS

http://museosorolla.
mcu.es

✚ H4

✉ Paseo del General
Martínez Campos 37

☎ 91 310 15 84

🕐 Tue–Sat 9.30–8,
Sun 10–3

🚇 Iglesia, Rubén Darío,
Gregorio Marañón

🚌 5, 14, 16, 27, 45, 61,
147, 150

♿ Few

💷 Inexpensive. Free to
under 18s, EU citizens over
65, Sat 2–8pm

More to See

BOTERO STATUES

In 1994, a section of Castellana was devoted to an exhibition of sculptures by 20th-century sculptor Fernando Botero. When the exhibition ended, *madrileños* retained a *Hand* in the middle of Castellana; the *Reclining Woman* in Calle Génova; and *Man on a Mule* in the Plaza de Colón.

✚ G/H3 ✉ Plaza de San Juan de la Cruz
🚇 Colón, Nuevos Ministerios 🚌 7, 14, 27, 40, 147, 150

CASA DE LAS SIETE CHIMENEAS

Legend has it that Philip II built the House of the Seven Chimneys in the 1580s for one of his mistresses, who is said to haunt it. During restoration, a woman's skeleton was discovered with coins nearby from Philip II's time.

✚ G7 ✉ Plaza del Rey 🚇 Banco de España
🚌 1, 2, 74, 146

FUNDACIÓN JUAN MARCH

www.march.es

One of Europe's most important private art foundations, this is home to some 30 major annual exhibitions. These have focused on Picasso, Kandinsky and Matisse.

✚ J5 ✉ Calle Castelló 77/Calle Padilla 36 ☎ 91 435 42 40 🕐 Mon–Sat 11–8, Sun and public hols 10–2. Closed Aug and between exhibitions. Free guided tours during exhibitions, telephone for details
🚇 Nuñez de Balboa 🚌 29, 52 ♿ Very good 🖐 Free

IGLESIA DE SAN ANTÓN

Designed by Pedro Ribera and built by Juan de Villanueva, this example of baroque architecture houses a magnificent art collection, including Goya's *The Last Communion of Saint José de Calasanz*, painted between 1775 and 1780, and architect Ventura Rodríguez's *Dolphins* statue.

✚ G6 ✉ Hortaleza 63 ☎ 91 521 74 73
🚇 Tribunal, Chueca

MUSEO DE ESCULTURA AL AIRE LIBRE

Connecting the *calles* Juan Bravo and Eduardo Dato is a road bridge over the Paseo de la Castellana.

Hand sculpture in the middle of Paseo de la Castellana

Underneath is an open-air display of sculpture by Spanish artists.

🞣 H4 ✉ Paseo de la Castellana 41
🚇 Rubén Darío 🚌 5, 14, 27, 37, 45

MUSEO NACIONAL DE CIENCIAS NATURALES

www.mncn.csis.es

The Natural Sciences Museum, founded in 1771, houses collections that encompass every branch of the natural sciences, from fossils to birds, mammals and reptiles. Each category is arranged by themes over five floors, and there are hands-on and interactive exhibits. Temporary shows cover everything from dinosaurs to the latest advances in DNA techniques for dating.

🞣 H3 ✉ Calle José Gutiérrez Abascal, 2
☎ 91 411 13 28 🕐 Sep–Jun Sat 10–8, Tue–Fri, Sun and public hols 10–5; Jul–Aug Tue–Fri, Sun and public hols 10–5, Sat 10–3
🚇 Gregorio Marañón, Nuevos Ministerios, Ríos Rosas 🚌 7, 12, 14, 27, 40, 45, 147, 150 ♿ Moderate ❓ Guided tours can be arranged in advance 💰 Moderate. Free under 4s and over 65s

MUSEO DEL ROMANTICISMO

www.museoromanticismo.mcu.es

This monument to faded romantic glory, founded in 1924, is inside mid-18th-century *madrileño* building that was the home of the traveler-painter the Marqués de Véga-Inclán. Though the content might be too sentimental for some, there are many items of interest, particularly Alenza's miniature *Satires of Romantic Suicide,* Goya's *Saint Gregory the Great,* and fine Isabelline and Imperial furniture.

🞣 G6 ✉ Calle San Mateo 13 ☎ 91 448 10 45/91 448 01 63 🕐 May–Oct Tue–Sat 9.30–8.30, Sun 10–3; Nov–Apr Tue–Sat 9.30–6.30, Sun 10–3 🚇 Tribunal 🚌 21, 37 ♿ Very good 💰 Inexpensive. Free under 18s, EU citizens over 65, from 2pm on Sat

PASEO DE LA CASTELLANA

Running in an almost straight line from Colón for 6.5km (4 miles) to Plaza de Castilla, the Castellana is one of Madrid's main points of reference and a center of business and nightlife. It splits the city in two, and many major sights are on or around it.

Museo del Romanticismo

✚ H5 🚇 Colón, Rubén Darío, Nuevos Ministerios, Lima, Cuzco, Plaza de Castilla
🚌 5, 14, 27, 40, 45, 147, 149, 150

PLAZA DE DOS DE MAYO

2 May 1808 is one of the most famous dates in Madrid's history. It was during the French occupation and a young girl, Manuela Malasaña, was shot by French soldiers for smuggling a weapon—actually just a pair of scissors. Earlier in the day, two locals, Velarde and Daoiz, led an attack on the Monteléon artillery barracks to capture arms. The insurgency was quashed, but sparked a four-year-long struggle for independence. The area is called Malasaña in memory of the heroine, and the dramatic statue here honors the two soldiers who died leading the uprising. Today, the square is lined with small bars and restaurants. Each year, on 2 May, Madrid commemorates that fateful day, with its hugely popular festival of parades ending with a classical concert.
✚ F5 🚇 Bilbao

SALA DEL CANAL DE ISABEL II

Considered one of Madrid's finest examples of industrial architecture, this display space, built between 1907 and 1911, hosts frequent concerts and excellent exhibitions.
✚ F3 ✉ Calle Santa Engracia 125 ☎ 91 445 10 00 🕐 Tue–Sat 11–2, 5–8.30, Sun and public hols 11–2 🚇 Ríos Rosas 🚌 3, 12, 21 149 💷 Free

SANTA BÁRBARA (LAS SALESAS REALES)

Probably the grandest, if not the most attractive, of Madrid's churches, Las Salesas was commissioned by Bárbara de Braganza, the wife of Fernando VI. It has an elaborate facade built between 1750 and 1758 by Carlier and Moradillo, and contains Sabatini's tomb of Fernando VI (1713–59). The adjoining monastery is currently the home of the Palacio de Justicia, or Madrid's Supreme Court.
✚ G6 ✉ Calle del General Castaños 2 ☎ 91 319 48 11 🕐 Daily 5–7pm; and for Mass 🚇 Alonso Martínez, Colón

Paseo de la Castellana (▷ 89)

A Walk North from Sol

Backstreets and boulevards, an arts center and the up-and-coming area of Malasaña: all are part of this walk.

DISTANCE: 4.6km (2.8 miles) **ALLOW:** 3 hours

START

PUERTA DEL SOL
✚ F7 🚇 Sol

END

GRAN VÍA
✚ F7 🚇 Gran Vía

❶ Leave the Puerta del Sol on the northwest side, on the pedestrianized Calle de Preciados. At the Plaza de Callao, bear left on the Gran Vía and follow it, past office blocks and cinemas, to the Plaza de España.

❼ Exit the square on Calle de Velarde and walk to Calle de Fuencarral. Follow this past the Museo Municipal, currently under renovation, all the way down to Gran Vía.

❷ Sit on a bench, enjoy the shade and pay your respects to Cervantes, Don Quixote and Sancho Panza, whose statues are at the far side of the square.

❻ Turn right on Calle de Ruiz and walk down to the Plaza del Dos de Mayo. All around is the Malasaña area, whose little streets are full of tiny shops, bars and clubs.

❺ Turn left on Calle de San Bernardo, walk uphill and cross over at the pedestrian crossing. Follow Calle de Divino Pastor, with its little old-fashioned shops and popular bars.

❸ Now walk up the hill on the Calle de Princesa, into a more residential area. Cross over to the Plaza de Cristino Martos, walk through this small square and follow Calle de Conde Duque, past the huge Cultural Center that used to be in service as an army barracks.

❹ Turn right on Calle de Montserrat, immediately right on Calle de Amaniel and stroll through the Plaza de las Comendadoras. Exit the little square on Calle de Quinoñes.

CHUECA AND THE NORTH WALK

Shopping

ABC SERRANO SHOPPING CENTER

www.abcserrano.com

The tiled exterior of what were the ABC newspaper offices now hides a veritable Aladdin's cave of boutiques. With over 30 to choose from, this is a place to relax and check out the baby clothes and wine, the high fashion and fun jewelry. Good restaurants on site.

🞢 H4/5 ✉ Calle de Serrano 61/Castellana 34 ☎ 91 577 50 31 🚇 Rubén Dario, Nuñez de Balboa, Serrano

ALMIRANTE 23

www.almirante23.net

This fascinating shop is a treasure-trove of old toys, posters boxes and bottles, comics, prints and much more besides. Take your time to browse, it's a great place to look for inexpensive take-home gifts and souvenirs.

🞢 H6 ✉ Calle Almirante 23 ☎ 91 308 12 02 🚇 Chueca

CACAO SAMPAKA

This could be Madrid's most tempting shop. Sampaka sells bars of chocolate as other shops sell silk ties. But it is not just bars. There are books and biscuits, jars and moulds, drinking chocolate and decorations. And the bar-cum-tasting room serves chocolate drinks, mousses, pastries and desserts.

🞢 H6 ✉ Calle de Orellana 4 ☎ 91 319 58 40 🚇 Alonso Martínez

HOMELESS

www.hossintropia.com

This boutique was founded in 1994 in San Sebastian as a fund-raising venture for the homeless. It now has its own label, 'HOSS'. The designs are casual, but stylish, aimed mainly at young professionals. There's another branch in the Salamanca district (Calle Serrano 16).

🞢 F6/7 ✉ Calle Fuencarral 16 ☎ 91 524 17 28 🚇 Gran Via

IOLI

Leather shoes and bags, silk hats and purses, all in vivid colors, all designed and made by Cynthia Ioli, the Argentine owner of this tiny shop. Women's shoes can be made to measure.

NEW MADRID FASHION

Though not yet Paris, Rome, London or even Barcelona, Madrid is slowly gaining a foothold in the world of men's and women's fashion. The international success of Adolfo Domínguez has been followed by that of Roberto Verino, and together with the avant-garde designs of Agatha Ruiz de la Prada and Jesús del Pozo, the Spanish designers are proving a serious threat to more established Italians. The beau monde does much of its shopping in the *barrio* Salamanca.

🞢 F6 ✉ Calle del Espiritu Santo 1 ☎ 91 521 00 22 🚇 Tribunal

MERCADO DE FUENCARRAL

www.mdf.es/madrid

Three floors and an outside area dedicated to the youth market. If you are looking for something different in fashion, leisure and culture, this is it: live DJs, hairdressers, tattoo parlors and loads of clothing, jewelry and gifts.

🞢 F6 ✉ Calle de Fuencarral 45 ☎ 91 521 41 52 🚇 Tribunal, Chueca, Gran Via

PURIFICACIÓN GARCÍA

www.purificaciongarcia.com

The sleek look, one of the trademarks of this distinguished Spanish designer of prêt-à-porter men's and women's clothing, is reflected in the minimalist layout of the store.

🞢 E8 ✉ Calle de Serrano 28 and 92 ☎ 91 435 80 13/576 72 76 🚇 Serrano

RESERVA Y CATA

www.reservaycata.com

Don't miss this excellent *bodega* (wine store) in a Chueca basement, offering some 600 different wines of mainly Spanish origin. Staff are knowledgable and on hand to help you choose the perfect bottle of wine for your occasion.

🞢 G6 ✉ Calle de Conde de Xiquena 13 ☎ 91 319 04 01 🚇 Colón

Entertainment and Nightlife

AREIA COLONIAL CHILL OUT

www.areiachillout.com
The place to relax where DJs perform nightly; cocktails and exotic snacks, too.
➕ G6 ✉ Calle de Hortaleza 92 ☎ 91 310 03 07 ⏰ 2pm–3.30am Ⓜ Tribunal

BAR CAFÉ DEL FORO

Though it does stage straight rock, the Café del Foro also has salsa, fusion and cabaret. Friendly and buzzing venue.
➕ F5 ✉ Calle San Andrés 38 ☎ 91 445 37 52 Ⓜ Bilbao

BUHO REAL

www.buhoreal.com
You might see the next up-and-coming international act right here at the city's 'Royal Owl'.
➕ G6 ✉ Calle Regueros 5 ☎ 91 308 48 51 ⏰ Concerts start at 9.30pm, closing times vary Ⓜ Alonso Martinez

CAFÉ MANUELA

After being wowed by the decor, visitors usually find the congenial atmosphere here well suited to writing postcards or chatting to friends. Occasional live entertainment—music concerts, poetry readings, exhibitions by local artists.
➕ F6 ✉ San Vincente Ferrer 29 ☎ 91 531 70 37 Ⓜ Tribunal

CAFÉ LA PALMA

www.cafelapalma.com
A cross between a conventional café, a wine bar, a Moroccan tea shop and a nightclub. The music in La Palma is just as eclectic—everything from rock 'n' roll to flamenco and Cuban fusion.
➕ F6 ✉ Calle de la Palma 62 ☎ 91 522 50 31 ⏰ Daily from 4pm Ⓜ Noviciado

CAFÉ RUIZ

A relatively peaceful retreat from the night-time mayhem of surrounding Malasaña, the Ruiz retains a late 19th-century feel and serves cocktails as well as coffee and milkshakes.
➕ F5 ✉ Calle Ruiz 11 ☎ 91 446 12 32 Ⓜ Bilbao

EL CLANDESTINO

Close to the Plaza de Chueca, this may look like just another small night club, but it has a reputation for showcasing great bands for its live music, usually jazz.

CHUPITO

Don't be surprised if, at the end of a meal in a restaurant, your waiter offers you a *chupito*. Usually served in a shot glass, a *chupito* is small but strong: *orujo de hierbas* (a yellow or green herb liquor), *ponche caballero* (spiced orange brandy), *pacharán* (sloe gin). This is on the house, helps to digest the meal and sends you on your way in a happy frame of mind.

➕ G6 ✉ Calle del Barquillo 43 ☎ 91 521 55 63 ⏰ Thu–Sat 1pm–3am Ⓜ Chueca

DEL DIEGO

Del Diego's superb design and highly attentive bar staff have quickly made it one of Madrid's big three *coctelerías*, along with El Chicote and Le Cock, two minutes away. This is the place to be and be seen.
➕ G7 ✉ Calle de la Reina 12 ☎ 91 523 31 06 Ⓜ Gran Vía

FORTUNY

www.palacetefortuny.com
Glitzy nightclub favored by media celebrities. This former palace's terrace garden is its best feature. A strict dress code applies here and there is a reputable restaurant.
➕ H4 ✉ Calle de Fortuny 34 ☎ 91 319 05 88 ⏰ Closed lunch Sat, Sun in winter Ⓜ Bilbao

OJALÁ AWARENESS CLUB

A typical example of the café clubs in Malasaña, this is fun upstairs (movies projected onto walls) and even more fun downstairs, where sand on the floor re-creates summer beach parties. Drinks and snacks are served all day; dinner in the evening.
➕ F6 ✉ Calle de San Andrés 1 ☎ 91 523 27 47 ⏰ 11am–midnight, later at weekends Ⓜ Noviciado, Tribunal

Restaurants

BAZTÁN (€)

An ideal spot to learn more about Spain's best wines, this is a new bar in an old taberna, overlooking the historic Plaza del Dos de Mayo. Tapas and other well-prepared snacks.

F5 ⊠ Calle de San Andrés 14 ☎ 91 523 25 73 🕒 Noon–midnight, later at weekends. Closed Mon 🚇 Tribunal, Bilbao

EL BIERZO (€)

www.restauranteelbierzobar-bieri.com

Lunch is excellent value at this down-to-earth and typical Madrid eating house, with two different set menus, featuring a choice of five or 10 dishes. There's more in the evenings, with well-sourced, fresh produce simply cooked—the range of different tortillas are well worth trying. Home-style desserts.

G6 ⊠ Calle Barbieri 16 ☎ 91 531 91 10 🕒 Mon–Sat 1–4pm, 9–11.30pm 🚇 Chueca

CASA MANOLO (€–€€)

www.casamanolomadrid.com

Whether you're looking for a good value lunch or a Madrid specialty, this traditional restaurant is a good choice. As well as dishes such as *cocidas* (Madrid casserole), good steaks or *bacalao* (dried cod) they also serve imaginative mixed salads with a Spanish twist and combination dishes where the choice is made for you.

G6 ⊠ Calle Orellana 17 ☎ 91 308 73 78 🕒 Tue–Sat 1.30–4.30, 9pm–midnight, Mon 1.30–4.30 🚇 Alonso Martinez, Colon

MERCADO DE SAN ANTÓN (€–€€€)

www.mercadosananton.com

Since its opening in 2011 this covered market has drawn in food fans from far and wide. Browse the ground floor outlets, selling a huge range of impeccably sourced produce, before heading for the first floor, with its numerous tapas bars, or the restaurant on the uppermost floor with great rooftop views.

G6 ⊠ Calle Augusto Figuero 24 ☎ 91 330 07 30 🕒 Market: Mon–Sat 10–10; bars: daily 10–midnight 🚇 Chueca

PEDRO LARUMBE (€€€)

www.larumbe.com

On the top floor of the ABC Serrano, this restaurant is theatrical and luxurious, ideal for that special occasion. Well-known chef Pedro Larumbe uses lobster and asparagus, foie gras and duck for the well-heeled clientele who live nearby. Well-priced wines.

H4/5 ⊠ Calle de Serrano 61, 4th floor ☎ 91 575 84 20 🕒 Closed Sat lunch, Sun 🚇 Rubén Dario, Nuñez de Balboa, Serrano

LA SACRISTÍA (€€)

www.la-sacrista.es

This restaurant is a popular haunt of local actors and directors, and is particularly well-known for its *bacalao* (cod) dishes. It also serves excellent steaks and *gambas* served dramatically flamed in whisky.

G7 ⊠ Plaza Vázquez de Mella 1 ☎ 91 522 09 45 🕒 Closed Sun 🚇 Gran Via

To the north of central Madrid are two of the city's great stadiums, the bullring and Real Madrid football club's Bernabéu Stadium. And within an hour or so of the city are some of the most historic and beautiful cities in Spain.

Cuatro Torres

Estación
de Chamartín

**Puerta de Europa
(Torres Kio)**

TETUÁN

**Real Madrid
Estadio Santiago
Bernabéu**

CHAMARTIN

**Aquópolis San
Fernando de Henares,
Los Caprichos Alameda
de Osuna**

Aeroporto
de Madrid-
Barajas

AVENIDA DE AMERICA

A2

CHAMBERÍ

PASEO DE LA CASTELLANA

**Plaza
de Toros**

M30

M110

SALAMANCA

PASEO DE LA CASTELLANA

Parque Quinta
Fuente del Berro

M23

MADRID

RETIRO

Parque
del
Retiro

AVENIDA DE LA PAZ

M30

CENTRO

Faunia

Estación
de Atocha

A3

AVENIDA DEL
MEDITERRÁNEO

ARGANZUELA

M30

Parque
Cerro
del
Tío Pío

M203

Parque
Enrique
Tierno
Galvan

M30

PUENTE DE
VALLECAS

USERA

A4/E05

**Warner Bros
Park**

Estación
Entrevías

Plaza de Toros

Plaza de Toros (left); spectators watching a bullfight (right); a matador (opposite)

THE BASICS

www.las-ventas.com

🚇 M5

✉ Avenida de los Toreros, Calle de Alcalá 237

☎ Museum 91 725 18 57; Stadium 91 356 22 00

🕐 Museo Taurino: Mar–Oct Tue–Fri 9.30–2.30, Sun, public hols 10–1; Nov–Feb Mon–Fri 9.30–2.30

🚇 Ventas

🚌 12, 21, 38, 106, 110, 146

♿ None

❓ Audioguides Mon–Fri 10–6; guided 45-min tours in English Mon–Fri 10–2

✋ Museo Taurino free

HIGHLIGHTS

● Bullfighting costumes in the museum—'suits of lights' may contain 5kg (11 pounds) of gold embroidery

● A papal bull in the museum (1567), which bans bullfighting

● Portrait of Joaquín de Rodrigo, attributed to Goya

● Highlight of the season is in May, during the *Feria San Isidro,* when some 30 bullfights take place

Is bullfighting art or blood sport? Whatever your feelings, you cannot help but be impressed by the world's most important bullring, the place in which a bullfighter must triumph if he is to achieve international recognition.

History and architecture The 1930s bullring is Madrid's finest example of neo-Mudéjar architecture, a style that resurfaced during the 19th century in imitation of the Mudéjar architecture of the 13th and 14th centuries and is defined by an interesting use of brickwork and bright ceramic tile inlay. In the square in front of the bullring is a melodramatic statue in memory of bullfighter José Cubero, inscribed with the words 'a bullfighter died, and an angel was born.'

Museo Taurino Half an hour in the stuffy Museo Taurino, next to the stables, gives you a basic overview of the famous names in bullfighting, if not of the complex art of bullfighting itself. Massive heads of legendary bulls and portraits of great bullfighters line the walls, and there are several dramatic portrayals of bull-runs, including a notable one by Mariano Benlliure (1862–1947). The highlights are the *trajes de luces* (suits of lights), as they are known, among them one belonging to Juanita Cruz, an early-20th-century woman bullfighter who was never allowed to fight on Spanish soil, and another worn by Manolete, perhaps the greatest of them all, who died in the ring in 1947. The museum displays are labeled in both Spanish and English.

Real Madrid

El Estadio Santiago Bernabéu is Real Madrid's home ground

Realmadrid
CLUB DE FUTBOL

THE BASICS

www.realmadrid.com

H1

Calle Conche Espina 1

Stadium: 91 398 43 70; tickets: 902 31 17 09

Guided tours in English from Gate 7, Mon–Sat 10–7, Sun, public hols 10.30–6.30. No tours 5 hours before match. Sala de Trofeos Tue–Sun 10.30–7.30; closed 3 hours before match

Café on site

Santiago Bernabéu

14

Good

Tour expensive, trophy room moderate

Founded in 1902, 'Real'—or Royal—rose to become one of the world's most famous football clubs. Its impressive achievements were officially recognized by FIFA, the world governing body, in 1988, when it was awarded the accolade 'the best club in the history of football'.

El Estadio Santiago Bernabéu Real Madrid have their home in the Santiago Bernabéu stadium. The stadium was inaugurated as the Estadio Chamartín (after the old stadium) in 1947, but the name was changed in 1955 in honor of the club's president. Today it holds more than 80,000 spectators, although before UEFA ruled that all standing places had to be converted to seats it held well over 100,000. In 1982, the stadium had perhaps its greatest hour, when it hosted the World Cup Final (when Italy beat Germany 3–1).

HIGHLIGHTS

● The massive world-famous stadium

● The Trophy Room, with its World and European silverware

● The new Realcafé Bernabéu, with its views

● Any home match, with passionate fans

● The club shop, with its array of replica shirts

● The stadium tour

Museum Even if you can't get to a game, you can take a guided tour of the stadium. You will get to enjoy a panoramic view of the inside of the stadium, the pitch and players' tunnel, the away dressing room and the Trophy Room. Unsurprisingly, given the club's illustrious history, this is packed with silver trophies. Numerous video screens show clips from great matches of the past, including *los blancos'* record nine European Cup triumphs between 1956 and 2002, as well as 18 Spanish cups and 32 Spanish League championships. Success is not limited to football: Real participates in many sports, notably basketball.

More to See

AQUÓPOLIS

www.aquopolis.es

Spanish children beg their parents to take them to Aquópolis, the biggest and best of the Madrid water parks and one of the largest in Europe. There are huge water slides, an adventure lake and wave machines. There is another Aquópolis, at San Fernando de Henares, 15km (9 miles) east of Madrid. There are rides, a lake and trees for shade.

➕ Off map ✉ Villanueva de la Cañada. Carretera de El Escorial km25 ☎ 902 34 50 06 🕐 Jun, Sep 12–7; Jul–Aug 12–8 🍴 Cafés 💲 Expensive

At San Fernando de Henares: ➕ Off map ✉ Carretera Nacional II ☎ 902 34 50 22 🕐 Jun, Sep 12–7; Jul–Aug 12–8 💲 Expensive

LOS CAPRICHOS DE ALAMEDA DE OSUNA

This is the closest Madrid comes to a formal English garden. Though a fair distance out, it's a pleasant place to head to for a weekend stroll.

➕ Off map ✉ Paseo de la Alameda de Osuna 🚇 El Capicho 🚌 101, 105, 115

CUATRO TORRES

A line of four stunning skyscrapers dominates the northern part of the city. Two of them, Torre Caja de Madrid and Torre de Cristal, are the two tallest buildings in Spain, each standing at 250m (820ft). The towers can be seen from the entrance/exit to the Metro at Chamartín station.

➕ Off map ✉ Paseo de la Castellana 🚇 Chamartín, Begoña

FAUNIA

www.faunia.es

Europe's only theme park dedicated to nature and biodiversity. The eight pavilions, each of which re-creates a different ecosystem with the authentic sights, sounds, smells, flora and fauna, will amaze and delight. Experience a tropical rainstorm and find out what it's like to live in the Arctic.

➕ Off map ✉ Avenida de las Comunidades 28 ☎ 91 301 62 35 🕐 Open daily from 10am; hours vary according to season and day of week 🍴 Cafés 🚇 Valdebernardo 💲 Expensive

Water-park fun

PALACIO REAL DE EL PARDO

www.patrimonionacional.es

Set in a vast park northwest of the city, this former royal palace is usually referred to as El Pardo, after the hill where it stands. Originally a hunting lodge back in 1405, the palace was built for Carlos I and expanded by Carlos III and his architect, Sabatini, in the 18th century. It was home to General Franco for 35 years. Today, you can visit rooms decorated with fine tapestries designed by Goya and woven at the Real Fábrica de Tapices (▷ 77), as well as murals by Maella and Bayeu. Not to be confused with the nearby Palacio de la Zarzuela, the home of the Spanish royal family since 1962, which is not open to the public.

✚ Off map ✉ Calle Manuel Alonso, El Pardo ☎ 91 376 15 00 ⏰ Apr–Sep daily 10–8; Oct–Mar daily 10–6 🍴 Restaurants nearby 🚌 Línea Interurbana 601. By car 14km (8.5 miles) from central Madrid via the M-30, M-605 🖐 Expensive. Free Apr–Sep Wed, Thu 5–8pm; Oct–Mar Wed, Thu 3–6pm

PUERTA DE EUROPA (TORRES KIO)

These striking towers are named after the Kuwaiti Investment Office, which withdrew funding halfway through construction. The walls are angled inward at 15 degrees—more than that and they would collapse.

✚ Off map ✉ Plaza de Castilla 🚇 Plaza de Castilla 🚌 49, 66, 124, 149

WARNER BROS PARK

www.parquewarner.com

This huge theme park on the outskirts of Madrid opened in 2003. The park's five zones are all themed: Cartoon Village, Hollywood Boulevard, the Old West, Super Heroes and Warner Studios. Recent attractions include the family roller coaster ride, Correcaminos Bip Bip, and Yogi Bear in Polynesia.

✚ Off map ✉ San Martín de La Vega. NIV to km22, then M-506 and follow signs ☎ 902 02 41 00 ⏰ Hours vary from day to day (only open weekends in winter). Check before you visit 🍴 Cafés, restaurants 🚉 C3 from Atocha 🚌 412, 413 🖐 Expensive

Puerta de Europa (Torres Kio)

Excursions

EL ESCORIAL

Philip II's vast palace and monastery was built between 1563 and 1584 as his mausoleum. Apart from its political pedigree, it's also an architectural triumph, with impressive collections of objects and antiques.

The palace contains 16 courtyards, 2,673 windows, 1,200 doors and 86 staircases; 900m (2,952ft) of frescoes line the walls. Its power is breathtaking, and the clear mountain air has left its granite and blue roof slates looking extraordinarily new. Among the highlights are the monastery, the library and the mausoleum, the resting place of most Spanish monarchs since Charles V (1500–58).

THE BASICS

www.patrimonionacional.es
Distance: 60km (37 miles)
Journey time: 1 hour
☎ 91 890 59 02/03
🕓 Apr–Sep daily 10–8; Oct–Mar daily 10–6 (last admission 1 hour before closing)
🚉 Regular trains from Atocha
💶 Expensive. Free Apr–Sep Wed, Thu 5–8pm; Oct–Mar Wed, Thu 3–6pm. Guided visit (€7), audioguide (€4)

SEGOVIA

Segovia, perched on a lofty, rocky outcrop, was founded during the Iberian period and taken by the Romans in 80BC. Occupied by the Moors, it then reverted to the Christians in 1085, and now, nearly a millennium later, is a popular weekend destination for *madrileños* in search of fresh air and a traditional suckling pig lunch.

The first thing you will see is the Roman aqueduct (1st and 2nd centuries AD), with 165 arches and a total length of 814m (2,670ft). In the old town are the magnificent 16th-century cathedral, with its imposing flying buttresses, and the 14th-century Alcázar, or fortress, which was largely rebuilt as a Gothic fantasy in the 19th century and offers lovely views from the top. Segovia is well known as the capital of Castillian cuisine.

THE BASICS

www.segoviaturismo.com
Distance: 88km (55 miles)
Journey time: 2 hours
🍴 Candido, Plaza Azoguejo 5
🚌 La Sepulvedana bus line from Paseo de la Florida 11, near Príncipe Pío Metro station
🚉 From Chamartín station (very slow)
ℹ️ Plaza Mayor 10 (tel 921 46 03 34); Plaza Azoguejo (tel 921 46 67 20). From Plaza Azoguejo, free guided tours of the city in Spanish (English leaflet) Jul–Sep (but you must pay the entry fee to the monuments)

TOLEDO

Legendary Toledo, with its hilltop site and fascinating maze of winding streets and hidden patios, is one of the nation's most beautiful and legendary cities. It was the Spanish capital from 567 to 711, and from 1085 to 1561. In other words, it has played a decisive role in Spanish history for far longer than Madrid.

National Monument Between the 12th and 15th centuries, Moors, Jews and Christians lived here side by side, and its rich combination of Moorish, Christian and Jewish heritage inspired its designation as a National Monument. Highlights are the 13th-century cathedral, the synagogues, Santo Tomé, the Museo de la Santa Cruz (for El Greco paintings) and the Alcázar, founded in 1085.

Alcázar Every culture that has ruled Toledo built a fortress on this site, and all dominated the city's skyline, as does the present-day version. This rather austere fortress was built by Charles V in the 16th century. During the Civil War, owing to its strategic position, it endured a very destructive 70-day siege, and today it houses an army museum that concentrates on those dark days.

Catedral Toledo's cathedral, one of the world's finest Gothic buildings, took 267 years to erect (1226–1493). Among its treasures are a baroque marble, jasper and bronze altarpiece, and paintings by El Greco and Goya.

Judería Although only two of Toledo's original 10 synagogues stand today, there is still a surprising amount to see in the Jewish Quarter. The 14th-century Sinagoga del Tránsito, housing the Museo Sefardí, has a superb Mudéjar interior.

THE BASICS

www.toledo-turismo.com
Distance: 70km (45 miles)
Journey time: 1 hour 15 mins

🚌 Galeano International from Estación Sur, Méndez Álvaro

🚆 From Atocha, several every hour in summer, less frequent in winter. To avoid a steep climb take a bus up the hill

ℹ️ Paseo de la Rosa s/n (tel no 925 24 82 32) open daily 9.30–3. There is a hop-on, hop-off tourist bus that leaves from outside the AVE station (€€€)

FARTHER AFIELD EXCURSIONS

THE BASICS

www.aranjuez.com
Distance: 50km (31 miles)
Journey time: 1 hour
🚌 Estación Sur, Méndez Álvaro (tel 91 468 22 00)
🚆 Atocha (tel 902 24 02 02)
ℹ️ Plaza de San Antonio (tel 91 891 04 27).
Open Tue–Sun 10–2, 4–6 (summer); 10–1, 3–5 (winter)

Palacio Real
☎ 91 891 07 40
🕐 Daily 10–6.15 (summer); 10–5.15 (winter).
💵 Moderate. Free Wed for EU citizens

❓ A special Strawberry Train (Tren de la Fresa) runs on weekends from Madrid, from late April through June. The train departs from Atocha train station at 10.05, arriving in Aranjuez at 11; the return journey departs around 6pm. The ticket price includes a guided visit of the palace and gardens, as well as a bowl of strawberries en route (tel 902 22 88 22)

ARANJUEZ

An hour south of Madrid is a city known as much for a piece of classical guitar music as for its glorious royal palace. On the banks of the Tajo River, Aranjuez is green, leafy and cool.

Palacio Real This lush landscape inspired Joaquín Rodrigo (1901–99) to compose the romantic and hugely popular Concierto de Aranjuez. (He is buried in the town cemetery.) The setting also drew Spanish rulers from the heat of Madrid. Although Felipe II commissioned the first palace back in 1561, the Palacio Real de Aranjuez took ages to finish: what you see is from the 18th century. But this fairy-tale palace was well worth the wait, from the throne room with its red velvet to the gala dining hall with its impressive chandeliers, furniture, tapestries and sculptures. One vast room, the Sala de Porcelana, is filled with porcelain, a particular hobby of Carlos III. Outstanding works of art include Murillo's *Bautismo de Cristo* (Baptism of Christ), which covers the ceiling of the chapel.

Gardens Many gardening enthusiasts go to Aranjuez just to see the landscaped grounds around the palace, with their fountains, statues and walks: the Jardín del Príncipe (Prince's Garden), the Jardín de Isabel II, the Jardín de la Isla (the Island) and the Jardín del Parterre, designed by Boutelou in 1746, with fine cedar trees, magnolias and flowers.

Strawberries The whole town is a pleasure to visit, with its old houses and small palaces, many of which are still in private hands. The town is also famous for its strawberries: a day trip to Aranjuez to eat strawberries is a Madrid tradition.

On a budget or celebrating a special event? With family or just looking for a fun weekend away? Even if you want to stay right in the throbbing heart of Madrid, there is accommodation for all wallets.

Introduction

Spain's capital has a wealth of hotels, *pensiones* and *hostales*. If you arrive without a booking, there are accommodation services at the airport and main bus and train stations. Many upper-range hotels, geared to business travel, offer reduced rates at weekends and holiday periods, so it's worth asking about reductions.

Location

The main factor to think about is location. The most popular area for visitors is in the heart of the old town (south of Sol between Plaza Mayor and Plaza de Santa Ana); you can walk to many of the main sights from here. Other options include Recoletos, the Paseo del Prado or Salamanca. If you want to be right in the heart of the nightlife action, Malasaña and Chueca are good bets.

Types of Accommodation

Spanish hotels are classified, regularly inspected and awarded 1 to 5 stars (*estrellas*). *Hostales* are often hard to distinguish from small hotels and can be better value for money. They are graded from 1 to 3 stars; a 3-star *hostal* is generally on a par with a 2-star hotel. *Pensiones* are usually family-run with simple rooms and sometimes shared bathrooms. Larger establishments have their own restaurants but in smaller places you'll need to eat out. If you prefer self-catering, you can also hire apartments from €50 a night for one person; see websites such as gomadrid.com or madridman.com. It's worth paying for a room with air-conditioning; summer temperatures can exceed 40ºC (104ºF).

DISABLED ACCESS

Look for modern hotels if you require better access and specially adapted rooms (www.access-able.com). These range from the well-priced Ibis Centro, with two disabled rooms (www.ibis.com), to the luxury InterContinental Madrid (four rooms, www.ihg.com). The website www.laterooms.com lists rooms for people with disabilities. In Spanish, look for the word *minusválido* (disabled).

Budget Hotels

PRICES

Expect to pay up to €100 per night for two in a budget room.

BARBIERI INTERNATIONAL HOSTEL

www.barbierihostel.com
A backpackers' hostel (all ages are welcome here) near Plaza de Chueca, which provides accommodation in shared rooms of 2, 4 and 8 beds. Bathrooms are single sex. Other services include 24-hour reception and kitchen facilities.

⊕ G6 ⊠ Calle Barbieri 15 (2nd floor) ☎ 91 531 02 58 Ⓜ Chueca, Gran Vía

GALIANO RESIDENCIA

In a quiet location, the Galiano's 29 spacious rooms and old-world feel make it one of Madrid's better-kept secrets.

⊕ H5/6 ⊠ Calle de Alcalá Galiano 6 ☎ 91 319 20 00 Ⓜ Colón

HOSTAL ALASKA

www.hostalalaska.es
A hostal on the fourth floor of a building in a street off the Puerta del Sol. It has seven en-suite rooms, air-conditioning and free Wi-Fi access.

⊕ F7 ⊠ Calle Espoz y Mina 7 (4th floor) ☎ 91 524 92 08 Ⓜ Sol

HOSTAL CERVANTES

www.hostal-cervantes.com
Conveniently located on the street after which it is named, an easy walk from the Prado and Thyssen-Bornemisza. The 20 en-suite rooms have televisions, safes and hairdryers. Rooms can be reserved online.

⊕ G8 ⊠ Calle Cervantes 34 ☎ 91 429 83 65 Ⓜ Anton Martín, Banco de España

HOTEL RESIDENCIA PAZ

Some rooms of this hostal, on a quiet street, overlook a shady courtyard. It's very clean and the staff are very efficient and very friendly.

⊕ E7 ⊠ Calle Flora 4 (2nd floor) ☎ 91 547 30 47 Ⓜ Sol, Ópera

IBIS MADRID CENTRO

www.ibishotel.com
On the site of a famous theater, this is a practical and friendly 64-room hotel in Malasaña, one of the up-and-coming areas of the city. A good base location, with plenty of restaurants and bars nearby. Excellent breakfasts are served here.

⊕ F5 ⊠ Calle de Manuela Malasaña 6 ☎ 91 448 58 16 Ⓜ Bilbao

THINGS TO NOTE

It is worth remembering that, at the lower end of the scale, a good *hostal* may be more comfortable than a poor hotel. Remember: prices can vary according to season.

OLÉ INTERNATIONAL HOSTEL

www.olehostel.com
This Malasaña hostel (open 24 hours) has a good kitchen, common room with satellite TV and internet, and lockers for valuables. Linen and breakfast are included and towels are available.

⊕ F5 ⊠ Calle Manuela Malasaña 23 (1st floor) ☎ 91 446 51 65 Ⓜ Bilbao, San Bernardo

SAN LORENZO

www.hotel-sanlorenzo.com
The San Lorenzo is most notable for its soundproof windows. Decor is stylish and rooms comfortable.

⊕ G7 ⊠ Calle Clavel 8 ☎ 91 521 30 57 Ⓜ Gran Vía

SANTANDER

www.hotelsantandermadrid.com
An old building decorated in the classical style. Rooms are en-suite with air-conditioning and heating. No restaurant.

⊕ G7 ⊠ Calle Echegaray 1 (corner with Carrera de San Jerónimo 26) ☎ 91 429 95 51 Ⓜ Sol, Sevilla

TRAFALGAR

www.bestwesternhoteltrafalgar.com
The Trafalgar is in a residential area north of the center. All 48 rooms are decorated in modern style and equipped with satellite TV. There's a restaurant, bar and an indoor swimming pool.

⊕ F4 ⊠ Calle Trafalgar 35 ☎ 91 445 62 00 Ⓜ Iglesia

Mid-Range Hotels

ACIS Y GALATEA

www.hotelesglobales.com
A small (25-room), tasteful modern hotel out of the city hub in the direction of the airport and near the IFEMA international trade fair showground. The name and the interior decor theme are inspired by opera. Wi-Fi throughout.
✚ Off map ✉ Calle Galatea 6 ☎ 91 743 49 01 🚇 Canillejas

AROSA

www.hotelarosa.com
Very central, the 139-room Arosa has long been popular, particularly with families, and makes an excellent base.
✚ F7 ✉ Calle de la Salud 21 ☎ 91 532 16 00 🚇 Sol, Gran Vía

ASTURIAS

www.hotel-asturias.com
Convenient to the Puerta del Sol, the 175-room Asturias is close to the main sights and nightlife. Ask for an inside room if you're sensitive to noise.
✚ G7 ✉ Calle Sevilla 2 ☎ 91 429 66 76 🚇 Sevilla

CARLOS V

www.bestwesternhotelcarlosv.com
The 67-room Carlos V is clean and bright and is next to the Puerta del Sol. If you can get a room on the sixth floor, you will get a balcony.
✚ F7 ✉ Calle Maestro Victoria 5 ☎ 91 531 41 00 🚇 Sol

CONDE DUQUE

www.granhotelcondeduque.com
Located in an enclosed square, the 143-room Conde Duque is among the more peaceful hotels near the city center.
✚ F5 ✉ Plaza del Conde Valle Suchil 5 ☎ 91 447 70 00 🚇 San Bernardo

EUROPA

www.hoteleuropa.eu
A comfortable hotel in a good location right on the Puerto del Sol, and within easy walking distance of the main sights.
✚ F7 ✉ Calle del Carmen 4 ☎ 91 521 29 00 🚇 Callao

GREEN EL PRADO

www.pradohotel.com
In this lovely building, within easy reach of the Prado and the Santa Ana district, windows are double-glazed, ensuring a good night's sleep.
✚ G8 ✉ Calle Prado 11

☎ 91 369 02 34 🚇 Antón Martín, Sevilla

HOTEL T3 TIROL

www.t3tirol.com
A comfortable hotel in the Argüelles business district. It has recently been renovated and it now also caters to families with small kids. Keen shoppers will find this location convenient, as the El Corte Inglés department store is just opposite; Parque del Oeste is also nearby. Hotel amenities include parking, internet access and car rental facilities.
✚ D5 ✉ Calle Marqués de Urquijo 4 ☎ 91 548 19 00 🚇 Argüelles

INGLÉS

www.hotelvitaingles.com
The clean, 58-room, family-owned Inglés is pleasantly located in a maze of narrow streets within easy reach of many sights. Good value.
✚ G7 ✉ Calle Echegaray 8 ☎ 91 420 46 30 🚇 Sevilla

LAGASCA

www.nh-hotels.com
This 3-star hotel in the heart of the Salamanca district is near the Calle Serrano shops and many good restaurants. Opened in the early 1990s, its 100 rooms are plainly furnished with wooden floors and striking bathrooms. It also has parking.
✚ J5 ✉ Calle de Lagasca 64 ☎ 91 575 46 06 🚇 Velázquez, Serrano

MEDIODÍA

www.mediodiahotel.com
Opposite Atocha train station, the Mediodía is close to the Reina Sofía and the Prado, and is well connected by public transport. Rooms are spacious and simple and have private bathrooms.

➕ H9 ✉ Plaza Emperador Carlos V 8 ☎ 91 527 30 60 🚇 Atocha

MODERNO

www.hotel-moderno.com
This 3-star hotel is only moments away from the Plaza Mayor and the Puerta del Sol, and has particularly welcoming staff. All 97 rooms have air-conditioning and private bathrooms.

➕ F7 ✉ Calle del Arenal 2 ☎ 91 531 09 00 🚇 Sol

OPERA

www.hotelopera.com
Rather plain-looking hotel but an excellent location near the opera house. All 79 rooms have satellite TV, some have balconies overlooking old Madrid.

➕ E7 ✉ Cuesta de Santo Domingo 2 ☎ 91 541 28 00 🚇 Ópera

SENATOR GRAN VÍA

www.hotelsenatorgranvia.com
This city hotel has an interior that blends functionality and urban style. Rooms have a CD player, iron, free minibar (nothing stronger than beer), coffee-making equipment, cable TV and bathrobes. There's also a laundry and internet access.

➕ F7 ✉ Gran Vía 21 ☎ 91 531 41 51 🚇 Gran Vía

TRYP MADRID CHAMBERI

www.tryphotels.com
A 3-star, 72-room hotel with well-sized, air-conditioned rooms in the affluent Chamberí area. Popular with businesspeople during the week, there are attractive weekend rates for visitors. Useful for the Real Madrid stadium. Parking nearby.

➕ F3 ✉ José Abascal 8 ☎ 91 447 40 00 🚇 Canal, Alonso Cano, Río Rosas

ZENIT-ABEBA

www.hotelzenitabeba.zenitho-teles.com
This modern 4-star hotel is perfect for shoppers as it is just a stone's throw from Goya and Serrano streets. The decor is functional, but the rooms are comfortable and spacious. The restaurant serves traditional Spanish cuisine and opens for lunch and dinner.

➕ K4/5 ✉ Calle de Alcántara 63 ☎ 91 401 16 50 🚇 Diego de León

---

ROOM MATE HOTELS

HOTEL MARIO

www.room-matehotels.com
This was the first of four jolly, budget-priced hotels in the Room Mate hotel group. Mario is well placed, close to the Royal Palace and the Ópera. Fun designs, fun atmosphere.

➕ E7 ✉ Calle de Campomanes 4 ☎ 91 548 85 48 🚇 Ópera

Other Room Mate Hotels include:

HOTEL ALICIA

www.room-matehotels.com
What was a 19th-century shoe factory is now a 34-room, designer hideaway on the corner of the Plaza Santa Ana.

➕ F/G8 ✉ Calle del Prado 2 ☎ 91 389 60 95 🚇 Sol, Antón Martín

HOTEL LAURA

www.room-matehotels.com
36 stylish rooms, almost on the historic Plaza de las Descalzas, and close to the Plaza Mayor and more.

➕ F7 ✉ Travesía de Trujillos 3 ☎ 91 701 16 70 🚇 Callao, Santo Domingo, Ópera

HOTEL OSCAR

www.room-matehotels.com
In buzzy Chueca, the latest Room Mate hotel opened in 2007.

➕ G7 ✉ Plaza Vázquez de Mella 12 ☎ 91 701 11 73 🚇 Chueca

Luxury Hotels

CASA DE MADRID

www.casademadrid.com

A short walk from the Royal Palace, this exclusive hotel is owned by art historian and interior designer, Marta Medina Muro. Each room is exquisitely decorated and furnished.

E7 ⊠ Calle Arrieta 2 ☎ 91 559 57 91 �) Ópera

HOSPES

www.hospes.com

A new and romantic boutique hotel in a classic 1883 building, this is perfectly placed within walking distance of the Prado, the Thyssen-Bornemisza, the Retiro and shopping.

H7 ⊠ Plaza de la Independencia 3 ☎ 91 432 29 11 �) Retiro, Banco de España

HOTEL PUERTA AMÉRICA

www.hoteles-silken.com/hoteles-puerta-america-madrid/

Some19 architects/designers from 13 countries combined to create this major addition to the city's hotel scene. Expect 12 floors of vibrant colors, with a rooftop bar, black swimming pool and imaginative restaurant. Not centrally located, but close to Serrano shopping.

L3 ⊠ Avenida de América 41 ☎ 91 744 54 00 �) Cartagena

HOTEL URBAN

www.derbyhotels.com

Slick and cool, the hard edges of this contemporary city center retreat next to the Parliament building are softened by original and ancient Oriental, Latin American, African and Egyptian works of art. 96 designer bedrooms with all the latest gadgets; swimming pool. The chic Glass Bar is a popular rendezvous.

G7 ⊠ Carrera de San Jerónimo 34 ☎ 91 787 77 70 �) Sol, Sevilla

INTERCONTINENTAL MADRID

www.ihg.com/intercontinental

Grand and central, with lots of marble and glass, this is where businesspeople, politicians and film stars stay. Rooms and bathrooms are spacious and comfortable.

In summer, the courtyard garden restaurant has live music. Popular brunch on Sunday. Attractive weekend rates.

H4 ⊠ Paseo de la Castellana 49 ☎ 91 700 73 00 �) Gregorio Marañón

ME MADRID

www.mebymelia.com

In the heart of the action, in what was once the formal old Reina Victoria (where bullfighters always stayed) is now Madrid's hip and happening hotel. Expect all the usual luxuries, from 300-thread-count linen and down pillow-top mattresses to organic, all-natural products for the shower. Stardust is provided by the Midnight Rose restaurant and its owner, Rande Gerber, husband of Cindy Crawford. 192 rooms.

F8 ⊠ Plaza de Santa Ana 14 ☎ 91 701 60 00 �) Anton Martín

RITZ

www.ritzmadrid.com

Spain's first luxury hotel, opened in 1910, was built for King Alfonso XIII. It lives up to its name, with 167 luxurious rooms in belle époque style. Between spring and autumn there's a delightful terrace-restaurant. Afternoon tea, taken to the sounds of a pianist, harpist or classical guitarist, is a highlight.

H7 ⊠ Plaza de la Lealtad 5 ☎ 91 901 67 67 �) Banco de España

Madrid is easy to get to from anywhere in the world. Although very walkable, the city also has excellent public transport. The main thing is to understand the hours when *madrileños* work, eat and play.

Planning Ahead

When to Go

Because of its position high on the inland plateau, Madrid can have some of the most extreme weather conditions in central Spain. Spring, early summer and autumn are the best times to visit. Tourist crowds dwindle in winter, when the weather can be bitterly cold, with temperatures rarely above freezing during the day, and icy after dark.

TIME

Spain is six hours ahead of New York, nine hours ahead of Los Angeles, and one hour ahead of the UK.

AVERAGE DAILY MAXIMUM TEMPERATURES

JAN	FEB	MAR	APR	MAY	JUN	JUL	AUG	SEP	OCT	NOV	DEC
48°F	52°F	59°F	63°F	70°F	79°F	88°F	86°F	77°F	66°F	55°F	48°F
9°C	11°C	15°C	17°C	21°C	26°C	31°C	30°C	25°C	19°C	13°C	9°C

Spring (March to mid-June) vies with autumn as the most pleasant time of year, with clear skies and sunny days, though there may be showers.
Summer (mid-June to August) is hot and dry. Rain is unusual between June and October. July and August are particularly hot.
Autumn (September to October) has little rain, sunny days and moderate temperatures.
Winter (November to February) has dry, clear days and low temperatures.

WHAT'S ON

January *Cabalgata de Reyes* (5 Jan): A procession marks the Three Wise Men's arrival.
San Antón (17 Jan): Pets are blessed in the San Antón Church, Calle Hortaleza 63.
February *Carnival*: A week of processions and parties ends on Ash Wednesday with the ritual 'Burial of the Sardine' by the River Manzanares.
ARCO: International contemporary arts festival.
April *Semana Santa* (Holy Week): Hooded, shoeless, chain-dragging *penitentes* bear images of Christ and the Virgin on their shoulders.

On Holy Thursday, during the procession around La Latina, the entire *barrio* takes to the streets.
May *Labor Day* and *Madrid Day* (1–2 May): Concerts region-wide; the main venue is Plaza Mayor.
San Isidro (15 May): Nightly concerts in Plaza Mayor mark the week leading up to the saint's day of San Isidro.
June *San Antonio de la Florida* (13 Jun): Street party marks St. Antonio's feast day.
San Juan (23 Jun): Fireworks in the Retiro to celebrate the festival of St. John.

August *Veranos de la Villa*: Madrid's summer festival of music, dance, theater and more.
October *Festival de Otoño*: International performing arts festival (through November).
November *International Jazz Festival*: Venues all over the city.
December *Fiestas de Navidad*: Christmas lights, markets and crèches lead up to Christmas. Christmas fair in Plaza Mayor.
New Year's Eve: Thousands gather for the fireworks in the Puerta del Sol.

NEED TO KNOW PLANNING AHEAD

Madrid Online

www.spain.info
The official website for tourism in Spain, with pages in Spanish, English, German, French, Italian, Japanese and Chinese. Easy to navigate, with plenty of useful information.

www.spain.info/en_US
Aimed at the US market, this offshoot of the main portal has plenty of information, plus details of travel agents and tour operators that are Spain specialists. It also lists all the Spanish tourist offices in the United States.

www.munimadrid.es/www.esmadrid.com
The Ayuntamiento (city council) has two websites. The older version, ww.munimadrid.es is mainly for residents; www.esmadrid.com, with pages in English, French and other languages, is for tourists.

www.turismomadrid.es
The official site of the Comunidad de Madrid, the autonomous Region of Madrid. In Spanish and English, with pages in other languages, it also covers nearby places such as Segovia, San Lorenzo de El Escorial and Toledo. Excellent.

www.eldibuk.com
Choose which part of Madrid you want to explore, click on the map and up come listings for everything from restaurants and bars to shops. Fun and funky; designed for locals as well as tourists. Spanish and English.

www.ctm-madrid.es
Come to terms with getting around Madrid by browsing the official transport site covering buses and the Metro (in English).

www.lanetro.com/madrid
Even a modicum of Spanish will be enough to access probably the best and zappiest of the Spanish-language events and listings sites, covering music, clubs, films and restaurants.

GOOD TRAVEL SITES

www.fodors.com
A complete travel-planning site. You can research prices and weather; book air tickets, cars, and rooms; ask questions (and get answers) from fellow travelers; and find links to other sites.

www.renfe.es
The official site of Spanish National Railways, with an English-language option.

www.wunderground.com
Good weather forecasting.

INTERNET ACCESS

The number of internet hotspots in Madrid is rapidly increasing. You can go online from your laptop in Barajas airport, Chamartín station, and many cafés. You can find the nearest hotspot at www.boingo.com but Wi-Fi internet access has now also become a standard service of contemporary hotels. As an alternative, there are still a very few cybercafés left where you can surf on the computers provided. The easiest to find is Café Comercial but it's a fair walk from the city hub.

Café Comercial
➕ F5 ✉ Gta de Bilbao 7
☎ 91 521 56 55 🕐 Mon–Thu 7.30am–1am, Fri, Sat 8.30am–2am, Sun 10am–1am Ⓜ Bilbao

Getting There

● Anyone entering Spain must have a valid passport (or official identity card for EU nationals). Visa requirements are subject to change; check before making your reservations.

● As of 2007, passengers on all flights to and from Spain have to supply advance passenger information (API) to the Spanish authorities. Full names, nationality, date of birth and travel document details (a passport number), are required. This information is compulsory. Travel agents should be able to collect this information at the time of booking, or it can be given to staff at check-in desks.

● The limits for non-EU visitors are 200 cigarettes or 50 cigars, or 250g of tobacco; 1 liter of spirits (over 22 percent) or 2 liters of fortified wine, 2 liters of still wine; 50ml of perfume. Travelers under 18 are not entitled to the tobacco and alcohol allowances.

● The guidelines for EU residents (for personal use) are 800 cigarettes, 200 cigars, 1kg tobacco; 10 liters of spirits (over 22 percent), 20 liters of aperitifs, 90 liters of wine, of which 60 can be sparkling wine, 110 liters of beer.

All flights arrive at Madrid-Barajas Airport, 12km (7.5 miles) northeast of the city. There are four terminals: T1, T2, T3 and the newest, T4, which is used by major international airlines such as Iberia and British Airways. For more information on arrivals and departures from each of the terminals, go to www.aena-aeropuertos.es ☎ 902 40 47 04.

ARRIVING BY AIR

There are tourist information areas at the airport and leaflets with information about getting to Madrid from Barajas. All terminals are served by Metro station Aeropuerto (Line 8); trains run from 6am to 1.30am. Terminal one is a long walk from the Metro station so allow 10 minutes to reach it. All terminals are linked by the free AENA (airport) shuttle bus; transit time between terminals ranges from 2–8 minutes. A taxi from the airport to the middle of Madrid takes around 30 minutes and costs €25–€30. For more information on ground transport, look at www.aena-aeropuertos.es and www.metromadrid.es.

ARRIVING BY TRAIN

RENFE (www.renfe.es), Spain's national rail company, has two mainline stations in the city. Trains from northern Europe, France and Barcelona (including the high-speed AVE train) arrive on the north side of the city at Chamartín. Trains running to and from Portugal and the south of Spain (including the high-speed AVE train) use Atocha, close to the city center. Book direct on www.renfe.com or use RENFE's US agents (Palace Tours, 800-724-5120, www.palacetours.com/renfe). Booking direct is preferable and the RENFE site is explained at www.seat61.com. For more information, see www.turismomadrid.es and www.esmadrid.com.

ARRIVING BY BUS

Madrid is served from other parts of Spain by many private bus companies. Inter-city coach services arrive at the Estación Sur de Autobuses on Calle Méndez Alvaro, southeast of the city center. Buses from outside Spain (England, Portugal and France) also terminate here. For all bus information ☎ 91 468 42 00.

ARRIVING BY CAR

Drivers access Madrid via the Spanish system of toll motorways (*autopistas*) or highways (*autovías*). From France and the north, routes run along both the Mediterranean and Atlantic coasts then head toward Madrid; routes through the Pyrenees are slower but more scenic. Madrid is clearly signposted at all interchanges. From southern Spain, take the A-4 from Seville via Córdoba. From Portugal take the A-5 from Badajoz. All roads connect with the three ring roads circling Madrid: the M30, M40 and M45. Head for Paseo de la Castellana, Madrid's main artery—most central locations are easily reached from here.

SENSIBLE PRECAUTIONS

● Carry valuables in a belt, pouch or similar—not in a pocket. Be especially wary in the crowds around Plaza Mayor, Puerta del Sol and the Rastro.
● Do not keep valuables in the front section of your rucksack. If possible, wear your rucksack on your front on buses and trains.
● Be aware of street tricks around tourist attractions. These include distracting you in conversation, or spraying foam on your back and then offering to clean it off while someone else grabs your bag.

INSURANCE

Check your insurance coverage and buy a supplementary policy if necessary. EU nationals receive medical treatment with the EHIC (European Health Insurance Card), which should be obtained before traveling. Health and travel insurance is still advised.

VISITORS WITH A DISABILITY

General access in Madrid is patchy, but gradually improving. For getting around, buses and taxis are the best bet, although only the newest buses have facilities for people with disabilities. New buildings and museums have excellent wheelchair access, older attractions have yet to be converted, and churches are particularly difficult. English-language advice is available on www.access-able.com. FAMMA is the Spanish association that deals with all disabilities (in Spanish only, www.famma.org).

Getting Around

MAPS

Metro maps are available from the ticket counter.
Free maps of the city are readily available at tourist offices, hotels, train stations and the airport.
Metro platforms have street maps indicating which exit leads where.

BUSES

● The bus system is efficient and far-reaching, with regular scheduled services to all parts of the city and its suburbs.

● Finding your way is made easy, as the various routes and stops are shown at every bus stop on a plan.

● There are two types of buses—the standard red bus and the yellow microbus. Both operate between 6am and midnight, and charge €1.50 for each one-way ride in the city, though the *bono* or Metrobus ticket giving 10 rides costs €12.20 (see below).

● Night buses (known locally as *buhos*, meaning owls) operate from Plaza de Cibeles to many suburbs between midnight and 6am and the tickets cost the same as during the day. The night bus service is not as punctual as the daytime one.

● Bus information offices are located in Plaza de Cibeles and Puerta del Sol, where you can pick up route maps and schedules.

● For full bus information see www.emtmadrid.es.

METRO

● The Metro system is very reliable and the best way of getting around the city quickly.

● There are 13 lines, each with a different color and number shown on route maps and at stations.

● The Metro is constantly expanding and improving. Most of the new stations are on the outskirts of this fast-growing city, built to speed commuters to and from work. Most of all, the Metro is clean and safe for visitors.

● The system is split into zones, with most of it in Zone A, while the outlying areas and lines are in zones B1, B2 and B3.

● The two airport terminals are classed as a separate zone, for which a supplementary fee is charged.

● A single journey ticket (*sencilla*) within Zone A costs €1.50 (€1.90 for all zones), but you can get a Metrobus ticket, giving 10 rides, for €12.20.

• A tourist card (*abono turistico*) is also available for visitors, and can be for 1, 2, 3, 5 or 7 days. A 1-day pass costs €8.40 for Zone A, a 7-day pass €35.40, with reductions of up to 50 percent for children. You would need to make six Metro or bus trips a day for it to work out cheaper than a Metrobus ticket.

• Buy tickets (also valid for buses) from Metro stations, some newsagents and tobacconists.

• The Metro system runs from 6am to 2am; schedule information and a full Metro map are available from www.metromadrid.es (☎ 902 44 44 03), or from any station. Also see www.ctm-madrid.es, which has all the information in English as well as Spanish.

• Metro trains run about every 3 to 6 minutes from Monday to Friday; this extends to every 15 minutes after midnight, and there are slightly fewer trains on weekends.

• It's best to avoid the rush hours, generally 7–9.30am and 7–9pm, when it gets very busy.

TAXIS

• Official taxis are white with a diagonal red stripe. A green light on the roof shows when they are free.

• The standard base taxi fare is €2.30, with a charge of €1 for every further kilometer. There is a supplement payable on Sundays and holidays, and for certain destinations, such as the rail station, airport and bullring.

• Make sure the meter is turned on and set at the base fare for your journey.

• The major private taxi companies in Madrid are TeleTaxi (☎ 91 371 21 31) and Radio Taxi (☎ 91 447 32 32). You can book your taxi online at www.radiotaxigremial.com.

TRAINS

• Chamartín, north of Plaza de Castilla, is the terminus for northern destinations. It is linked by a through line with Atocha.

• *Cercanías* refers to local and suburban trains, *largo recorrido* to intercity and long-distance trains.

GUIDED WALKS

Official guided tours of the city leave regularly from the Madrid Tourism Center on Plaza Mayor 27. They go on foot, by bus and even by bicycle. There are 28 different themes, such as the Oldest Madrid, Madrid in Films, Great Writers and 20th-century Architecture.
For dates and times visit www.esmadrid.com. It is important to book ahead at the tourist office online or by phoning ☎ 90 222 14 24. Cost is €5.90 per person.

For a really special experience, get under the skin of Madrid on a tour run by the Spanish-American husband and wife team of Carlos and Jennifer Galvin, who run LeTango Tours. They take you to the places that locals go, explaining how various traditions began and why they persist. One of the most entertaining walks is a foodie-oriented 'tapas tour' (☎ 655 818 740, mobile 661 752 458, toll free US 1 866 866 5107; www.letango.com).

A British guide with a passion for the Duke of Wellington, Stephen Drake-Jones also runs the Wellington Society, devoted to understanding the history of Spain in general and Madrid in particular (mobile 609 143 203; www.wellsoc.org).

Essential Facts

NEED TO KNOW ESSENTIAL FACTS

● Municipal Lost Property Office (Oficina de Objetos Perdidos) ✉ Paseo del Molino 7 ☎ 91 527 95 90 🚇 Legazpi 🕐 Mon–Fri 9–2

● For objects lost on a bus: EMT ✉ Cerro de la Plata 4 ☎ 902 50 78 50 🚇 Pacífico 🕐 Mon–Fri 9–2. Ask for *objetos perdidos*.

● To claim insurance, you must obtain a *denuncia* (signed statement of loss) from a police station.

MONEY

The euro (€) is the official currency of Spain. Banknotes are in denominations of 5, 10, 20, 50, 100, 200 and 500 euros, and coins in denominations of 1, 2, 5, 10, 20, 50 cents and 1 and 2 euros.

ELECTRICITY

● The standard current is 220 volts.
● Plugs are of the round two-pin type.

ETIQUETTE

● Spaniards rarely form orderly queues, but are generally aware of their place in the service order.

● Smoking is officially banned in all public enclosed spaces in Spain, but some bars and restaurants have smoking areas, and a few hotels offer rooms for smokers.

● It is considered good manners to issue a general hello (*buenos días* in the morning; *buenas tardes* in the afternoon/evening) when entering a shop, office, etc. and to say goodbye (*adios*) when leaving.

● Speak up to attract attention in bars and restaurants. Say *Oiga* (Oy-ga, literally 'hear me'), and add *por favor* (please).

● When at a bar drinks are normally paid for before you leave the bar, not on a round-by-round basis.

● Tipping is discretionary, but 5 percent is normal practice.

MONEY MATTERS

● Most major travelers' checks can be changed at banks. American Express offers the best travelers' check rates.

● Credit cards are generally now accepted in all large establishments and also many smaller places.

● There are many multilingual ATM/cash machines.

OPENING HOURS

● Shops: 9–1.30, 5–8; department stores: 9–9. Some are open Sundays.
● Churches: 9.30–1.30, 5–7.30. Many only open half an hour before a service.
● Museums: many close on Mondays.
● Banks: Mon–Fri 9–2; between October and May many banks open also from 9–1 on Saturdays.

MAIL

● Buy stamps (*sellos*) from a post office (*oficina de Correos*) or tobacconists (*estancos*), indicated by a yellow and brown sign.

● Madrid's most central post office is at Paseo del Prado 1, ☎ 91 523 06 94 open Mon–Fri 8.30am–9.30pm Sat 8.30–2. There are other post offices at El Corte Ingles, Calle Preciados 1–4, Carrera de San Francisco 13 and Calle Jorge Juan 20.

● Post boxes are mostly yellow with two slots, one marked 'Madrid' and the other for every-where else (*Provincias y extranjero*).

TELEPHONES

● Public telephones take €1 and €2 coins and 2c, 5c, 10c, 20c and 50c coins.

● Phone cards are available from newsstands; some phones accept credit cards.

● The technology for mobile, or cell, phones in Spain is GSM, which may be incompatible with some countries, for example, the USA or Japan. Tri-band mobiles/cell phones will work. Check to make sure your phone will work and what the cost of calls will be. Charges for roaming—using your phone in another country—can be high.

● To call Spain from the UK dial 00 34 followed by 91 for Madrid and then the seven digit number. To call the UK from Spain dial 00 44 and omit the zero from the area code. To call Australia dial 00 61.

● To call Spain from the US dial 011 34 followed by 91 for Madrid and then the seven digit number. To call the US from Spain dial 001.

MEDICINES AND HEALTHCARE

● Pharmacies (*farmacias*) are indicated by a flashing green cross and are usually open 9.30–2 and 5–8. All post a list of *farmacias de guardia* (all-night chemists).

● Spanish pharmacists are qualified to give over-the-counter advice on healthcare and many minor ailments, but for serious conditions you should ask for directions to the nearest hospital or doctor's office.

EMERGENCY NUMBERS

● Police (Local) ☎ 092
● Police (National) ☎ 091
● Police (Guardia Civil) ☎ 062
● Police, Ambulance, Fire ☎ 112
● Fire station: Madrid ☎ 080
● SATE is a special 24-hour service for foreign tourists who need to report crimes to the police. In Spanish, English and French ☎ 90 210 21 12; www.es.madrid.com.

TOILETS

Gone are the days when tourists needed to worry about hygiene in toilets in restaurants and bars. Modern Spain has modern toilet facilities.

TOURIST OFFICES

Plaza Mayor 27 ☎ 91 454 44 10 🕐 Daily 9.30–8.30

Plaza de Colón ✉ Access through Paseo de la Castellana 🕐 Daily 9.30–8.30

Plaza de Cibeles ✉ Calle Bulevar (on corner with Paseo del Prado) 🕐 Daily 9.30–8.30

Paseo de Arte ✉ On corner with Glorieta de Carlos V 🕐 Daily 9.30–8.30

Madrid-Barajas Airport Terminal 2 and 4 ☎ 91 305 86 56 🕐 Daily 10am–11pm

Terminal 4 ☎ 902 10 00 07 🕐 Daily 10am–11pm

Language

English is now the second language of many, if not most, Europeans. Staff in Madrid's hotels, many restaurants and even many shops speak English. However, it is fun to try a few words in Spanish and, of course, any efforts are appreciated! In bars, the tapas on offer are often chalked up on a board; perfect for trying out your Spanish.

Pronunciation
c before an *e* or an *i*, and *z* are like *th* in thin
c in other cases is like *c* in cat
g before an *e* or an *i*, and *j* are a guttural sound which does not exist in English—rather like the *ch* in loch
g in other cases is like *g* in get
h is normally silent
ll is similar to y
y is like the *i* in onion
Use the formal *usted* when speaking to strangers; the informal *tu* for friends or younger people.

COURTESIES	
good morning	*buenos días*
good afternoon/ evening	*buenas tardes*
good night	*buenas noches*
hello (informal)	*hola*
goodbye (informal)	*hasta luego/hasta pronto*
hello (answering the phone)	*¿Diga?*
goodbye	*adiós*
please	*por favor*
thank you	*gracias*
you're welcome	*de nada*
how are you? (formal)	*¿Como está?*
how are you? (informal)	*¿Que tal?*
I'm fine	*estoy bien*
I'm sorry	*lo siento*
excuse me (in a bar)	*oiga*
excuse me (in a crowd)	*perdón*

USEFUL WORDS	
I don't know	*No lo sé*
I don't think so	*Creo que no*
I think so	*Creo que sí*
It doesn't matter	*No importa*
Where?	*¿Dónde?*
When?	*¿Cuándo?*
Why?	*¿Por qué?*
What?	*¿Qué?*
Who?	*¿Quién?*
How?	*¿Cómo?*
How much/ many?	*¿Cuánto/ cuántos?*
Is/are there?	*¿Hay?*
ticket	*entrada*

BASIC VOCABULARY

yes/no	sí/no
I do not understand	no entiendo
left/right	izquierda/derecha
entrance/exit	entrada/salida
open/closed	abierto/cerrado
good/bad	bueno/malo
big/small	grande/pequeño
with/without	con/sin
more/less	más/menos
hot/cold	caliente/frío
early/late	temprano/tarde
here/there	aquí/allí
today/tomorrow	hoy/mañana
yesterday	ayer
how much is it?	¿cuánto es?
where is the...?	¿dónde está...?
do you have...?	¿tiene...?
I'd like...	me gustaría...
I don't speak Spanish	no hablo español

FOOD

apple	manzana
banana	plátano
beans	habichuelas
chicken	pollo
clams	almejas
duck	pato
fish/ seafood	pescado/ marisco
fruit	fruta
lamb	cordero
lettuce	lechuga
lobster	langosta
meat	carne
melon	melón
orange	naranja
pork	cerdo
shrimp	gambas
squid	calamares
tomato	tomate
tuna	atún
turkey	pavo

IN THE RESTAURANT

smoking allowed	se permite fumar
no smoking	se prohibe fumar
menu	la carta
fork	tenedor
knife	cuchillo
spoon	cuchara
napkin	servilleta
glass of wine	copa
glass of beer	caña
water (mineral)	agua (mineral)
still	sin gas
sparkling/bubbles	con gas
coffee (with milk)	café (con leche)
May I have the bill/check	¿La cuenta, por favor?
Do you take credit cards?	¿Aceptan tarjetas de crédito?
tavern	mesón/taberna
cakes	pasteles
small snacks	pinchos
sandwiches	bocadillos
set dishes	platos combinados

SHOPPING

ATM/cash machine	cajero
I want to buy...	Quiero comprar...
belt	cinturón
blouse	blusa
dress	vestido
shirt	camisa
shoes	zapatas
skirt	falda
tie	corbata
gloves	guantes
socks	calcetines
small	pequeño
medium	mediano
large	grande
cotton	algodón
silk	seda
wool	lana
café	cafetería
breakfast	desayuno
lunch	almuerzo
dinner	cena

Timeline

BEFORE AD800

Iberian tribes inhabited Madrid from around 1000BC. The Romans ruled the Iberian peninsula between 218BC and the 5th century AD and Madrid became a stopping place.

In AD711, Muslims defeated the Visigoths—areas of Spain came under Muslim rule for 800 years.

854 Muhammad I of Córdoba founds the city of Madrid.

1083 Madrid is recaptured by Alfonso VI; Christians, Jews and Muslims all inhabit the city.

1202 Alfonso VIII recognizes Madrid as a city by giving it Royal Statutes.

1309 The Cortes, or Parliament, meets in Madrid for the first time.

1469 The marriage of Catholic monarchs Ferdinand and Isabella unites Aragon and Castile.

1492 The conquest of Granada completes the unification of Spain. Spain begins a 200-year period of imperial power, and expels the Jews.

1561 Philip II establishes Court in Madrid: a cultural 'Golden Age' begins.

1578 Philip III (1578–1621) is the first monarch to be born in Madrid.

1617–19 Plaza Mayor is built.

1759 Charles III begins a modernization schedule for Madrid.

1808–12 French occupation; famine kills 30,000. Spanish rule restored 1814.

Below, from left to right:
The interview of Columbus
with Queen Isabella;
Ferdinand the Catholic;
Philip II; statue of Philip
III in the Plaza Mayor;
General Francisco Franco;
statue of the painter Goya

1819 Prado museum opens.

1851 The Madrid–Aranjuez railway line is inaugurated.

1873 The First Republic is declared.

1917 Spain faces a general strike.

1919 The first Metro line in Madrid opens.

1931 The Second Republic is declared.

1936–39 The Spanish Civil War takes place, sparked by uprising in North Africa. The Nationalists win, and the long dictatorship of General Franco follows.

1975 General Franco dies; King Juan Carlos is declared his successor.

1977 The first democratic general election.

1986 Spain joins the EEC (now EU).

1992 Madrid is European City of Culture.

2002 Spain adopts the euro: a landmark in the move to mainstream Europe.

2008–14 Spain's recession bites hard in Madrid; despite this, the city is committed to a 'greener' future, epitomized by the Madrid Río project, a new 10-km (6.4-mile) long park along the Manzanares river.

MADRID PEOPLE

Charles III

Charles III is often known as 'the best mayor that Madrid ever had'. More than any other single historical figure, he is responsible for today's Madrid. He came to the throne in 1759 and was a keen proponent of Enlightenment ideals.

Cervantes

Cervantes is the author of *Don Quixote,* believed by some to be the first novel ever written. A tax collector, he wrote *Don Quixote* while in jail for manipulating accounts. He died in Madrid in 1616.

Goya

Goya (1746–1828) is the painter most readily associated with Madrid, though he neither was born nor died here. He settled in Madrid in 1774 and became Court painter to Charles IV in 1789.

GOYA

Index

Titles in the Series